SUMMA PUBLICATIONS, INC.

Thomas M. Hines
Publisher

William C. Carter
Editor-in-chief

Editorial Board

Benjamin F. Bart
University of Pittsburgh

William Berg
University of Wisconsin

Germaine Brée
Wake Forest University

Michael Cartwright
McGill University

Hugh M. Davidson
University of Virginia

Elyane Dezon-Jones
Washington University

John D. Erickson
Louisiana State University

Wallace Fowlie
Duke University
(emeritus)

James Hamilton
University of Cincinnati

Freeman G. Henry
University of South Carolina

Norris J. Lacy
Washington University

Edouard Morot-Sir
University of North Carolina, Chapel Hill
(emeritus)

Jerry C. Nash
University of New Orleans

Allan Pasco
University of Kansas

Albert Sonnenfeld
University of Southern California

Orders:
Box 20725
Birmingham, AL 35216

Editorial Address:
3601 Westbury Road
Birmingham, AL 35223

Marcel Proust's
A la recherche du temps perdu

Marcel Proust's
A la recherche du temps perdu

A Search for Certainty

Jack Louis Jordan

SUMMA PUBLICATIONS, INC.
Birmingham, Alabama
1993

Copyright 1993
Summa Publications, Inc.
ISBN 0-917786-97-1

Library of Congress Catalog Number 93-83302

Printed in the United States of America

All rights reserved.

Marcel Proust Studies
Vol. 3

Words move, music moves
Only in time; but that which is only living
Can only die. Words, after speech, reach
Into the silence. Only by the form, the pattern,
Can words or music reach
The stillness, as a Chinese jar still
Moves perpetually in its stillness.

. . . .

        These are only hints and guesses,
Hints followed by guesses; and the rest
Is prayer, observance, discipline, thought and action.

—T.S. Eliot, *Four Quartets*

Contents

Acknowledgments	ix
Introduction	1
I. Proust's Scientific Perspectives: A Critical Overview	5
II. Proust's Scientific Spectacles	13
III. Proust in Motion	29
1. Immobile Means of Transportation	31
2. Trains	40
3. Automobiles	49
4. Airplanes	53
IV. Proust and the Human Sciences	63
1. The Background	64
2. The Pathologist	69
3. The Naturalist	76
4. The Psychologist	82
Conclusion	109
Appendix	113
Notes	121
Bibliography	127

Acknowledgments

THIS BOOK COULD NOT have been written without the help of many people, both at Vanderbilt and at the University of Virginia. The fundamental ideas behind this study were conceived while I was studying at Vanderbilt. I owe my knowledge of phenomenology and the philosophy of science to Dr. John Compton of the Philosophy Department. His view of these two subjects provided me with the tools I needed in order to tackle a work like Marcel Proust's *A la recherche du temps perdu*.

I would also like to thank Dr. Alexander Marchant, a former professor of Vanderbilt's History Department. His expansive mental embrace of man's history and culture gave strength to my own sometimes uncertain synthesis.

Most of all I would like to thank M. Claude Pichois, whose dedication to, knowledge of, and enthusiasm for literature have inspired (and awed) me for almost twenty years. His patience and understanding over the years have helped me through more than one difficult moment. Simply thanking him for presenting me with the most important literary experience of my life would not begin to cover the debt I owe. Merci, maître.

The present structure of this book was developed while at the University of Virginia. First, and most importantly, I would like to thank Dr. A. James Arnold for his tireless efforts on my behalf. Without his clarity of thought, precision of expression and openness to new ideas, this study would not exist. His dedication to perfection is a model for any scholar. His diplomatic skills could set an example for any ambassador. I would also like to thank Jim Arnold's wife, Jo, whose behind the scenes support and suggestions helped give my work added impetus and direction.

I would like to thank Dr. Hugh M. Davidson, a gentleman and a scholar, a man who still believes in the importance of the questions being asked by scholars of all fields. Thanks to Dr. Davidson, I was given a rare opportunity to discuss my ideas with scholars from both the humanities and the sciences. He is, in the classic and the modern sense of the term, an "honnête homme."

My thanks must also be expressed to my family and friends, without whose patient support for my work over the years, I would not have made it.

—*J. L. J.*

Introduction

AS THE TITLE SUGGESTS, the underlying theme of this study assumes that there is an ongoing search in Marcel Proust's *A la recherche du temps perdu*. Proust's use of "recherche" in his title lends credence to this assumption. That it is a search not only for "lost time," but also for certainty implies a state of uncertainty which would necessitate such an undertaking. From the first pages of Proust's novel, as this study seeks to demonstrate, we shall see that this uncertainty is all-pervasive. It includes a loss of the basic realities of time, space and self, all of which serve to give meaning and order to an otherwise chaotic world. In following Proust's search we shall see his novel as a watershed, where the laws of Newton and Descartes dominated man's vision of the world and himself until the turn of the century, when developments in both technical and theoretical science shattered this world view. In each section of each chapter of this study we see the failure of the mechanistic, causal order to provide the certainty which for so long has made our world a comfortable, familiar place in which to live. The first chapter gives a critical overview of what different critics have seen as the fundamental imagery in Proust's novel. Each of the critics quoted has chosen to study essentially one aspect of science in Proust's novel: the developments in glass making and ocular science; botany; medicine; physics; or psychology. My purpose is rather to produce a synthesis which would provide a unified view of these different scientific perspectives and, thereby, to achieve a sense of the comprehensive cosmogony of the world Proust has created in his novel. This is, to say the least, a large undertaking. In both the sciences and the humanities we have seen fields of research narrowing in such a precise fashion as to make it difficult—if not impossible—for any discussion to take place even within their respective domains. To embark on a synthesis of various sciences, much less to incorporate them in a humanistic study, will inevitably draw the wrath of more than one specialist, be he (or she) from the sciences or the humanities. Indeed, Proust's own efforts to incorporate the sciences mentioned above into his novel have been criticized as "pseudo-scientific."

After all, Proust is an artist, not a scientist. Proust himself saw a certain irony in comparisons of the novelist to the scientist, as seen, for instance, in the "disjunction that is sometimes present between what Proust thinks and what the narrator says, by the attempt to 'recreate' rather than 'analyze abstractly' the evolution of thought."[1] However, is this all that can be said? Are the two disciplines so diametrically opposed? As we shall see in the chapters which follow, the delineation is not so clear-cut.

Both in its entirety and in the individual chapters the organization of this book reflects these changes in world views. The chapter which follows the critical overview concerns the study of the relation of subject and object as it is reflected by the developments in ocular science. The next chapter concerns the world external to man (Proust in Motion). In the final chapter, the search is turned inward toward man's internal world, his psyche.

The structure of the chapter concerning physics (Proust in Motion), reflects a movement outward which can be seen in Proust's novel. We first see Marcel immobile in his room, then moving about as a pedestrian, then travelling in trains and automobiles. The increase in the speed of locomotion finally incorporates the revolutionary changes brought about by the invention and spreading use of the airplane, resulting in a world view which has turned to the stars.

Whereas "Proust in Motion" is organized in a telescopic, outwardly oriented fashion, the following chapter, "Proust in Motion," is one which reflects the author's vision as he turns inward, focusing in on the essence of man. In this chapter a brief consideration of the background of this half of Proust's search precedes a study of man in his outward, physical nature. A section concerning man as species follows with, finally, a movement towards man's internal landscape, or his psyche. In this final section, a possible response is given to a second argument presented by some critics against Proust's use of "pseudo-scientific" references. His scientific allusions, this argument maintains, are only flimsy justifications of his own personal world view, both aesthetic and sexual. It is true that Proust's use of botanical imagery can be seen in letters written during high school to classmates such as Jacques Bizet and Daniel Halévy. His use of floral imagery to allude to sex in these letters does seem to support this argument (Rivers 57). Nonetheless it is true that Proust has indeed brought together all of the developments in science mentioned here to create the world of his novel. In *A la recherche du temps perdu,* Proust's scientific references have outgrown the boundaries of sexual justification to become an integral part of his aesthetic vision. His efforts to bridge the gulf between science and art reach far beyond a pseudo-scientific justification of homosexuality. As chapter four will show, by uniting two fundamental ways (scientific and mythic) of viewing man and nature, Proust creates a fundamental metaphoricity in his choice of archetypes. As Rivers notes: "But side by side with . . . scientific language we find the suggestion that we are reading not science but myth" (222). Together, in a metaphorically androgynous archetype they express "primal totality . . . a means of contacting the history of . . . the race" (Rivers 235).

The approach used here is based on an effort to develop the homology between Proust's novelistic art and science using what is essentially a phenomenological methodology. While acknowledging the virtues of the precision found in a more narrowly focused study, it is hoped that this work will offer a view of the world of Proust's novel which is itself well-founded, coherent, and original enough to make up for the admitted limitations inherent in its effort to reunite such apparently disparate fields of inquiry and expression as science and art. The purpose is not to prove that Proust was a scientist. It is an effort to show how Proust's embracing world view resulted in a metaphorically unified view of man and nature, the breadth of which has not been seen in the novel before or since.

All references to Proust's *A la recherche du temps perdu* are based on the 1954 edition prepared by Pierre Clarac and André Ferré. While a new edition has recently been published under the direction of Jean-Yves Tadié, and should be of great value to any future work done on Proust's novel, it had not been published in its entirety at the time of the writing of this study.

✦ ✦ ✦

I

Proust's Scientific Perspectives: A Critical Overview

THE DISCUSSIONS CONCERNING Proust's interests in science have been numerous and varied from the publication of *Du côté de chez Swann*. The origins of his interests in science, their influence on and manifestations in his work, have been debated by many critics, both early and late. The forms such criticism has taken have been equally varied—ranging from personal accounts, such as those given by his young friend Marcel Plantevignes, to a broader, more philosophical interpretation of the style of Proust's work, such as that written by Camille Vettard, in which he compares Proust to Einstein.

Any discussion of this nature must answer three basic questions. First, what is the definition of science—classical or modern, Newtonian or Einsteinian, technical or theoretical? In his work *Marcel Proust and His French Critics*, Douglas Alden discusses many of the earlier critics of Proust's work. In the chapter "The 'New Classicist,' " the importance of a definition of terms becomes apparent. Even among those critics who find him "scientific" there is disagreement. Is he "modern" or "classical" in his scientific approach? Is his work perhaps a watershed, containing both a classical, Cartesian, mathematical, rational, objective view, and a modern, subjective, intuitive attitude reflecting, in part, the emerging science of psychology? Can Proust's work even be regarded as "post-modern," suggesting developments in psychology and physics not directly connected to Proust's life but which can be said to be part of the spirit of the time (of which *A la recherche du temps perdu* may be seen to be a reflection)?

The second question to be answered is that of the origin of Proust's interest in and knowledge of a particular science or scientific attitude. Here one must step out of the work and study some of the aspects of Proust's life which influenced his "philosophy of science" and, ultimately, his view of art, man, and the world. The influences can be divided into three types. The first concerns those of the most direct nature (through family, friends, teachers, readings, etc.). The second sort of influence is more indirect, as will be seen in the comparisons of Proust to Freud and Schopenhauer. The last sort of influence is perhaps the most difficult to establish. Unlike the first two, this influence is more a manifestation of the spirit of the time, and establishing causal connections is not necessarily possible.

The third question returns us to the work itself. What is the relevance of a particular science to Proust's novel—perspective, style, imagery, characterization—and how does the scientific attitude (or attitudes) manifest itself in the world of his work?

Before turning to the influences on Proust's scientific attitude and their particular manifestations in *A la recherche du temps perdu* a brief look at what some critics have claimed as predominant images in the work should suggest both the importance and the variety of Proust's scientific interests.

For Roger Shattuck (*Proust's Binoculars*) optical imagery is predominant on every level of the work. It is "principally through the science and the art of optics that he beholds and depicts the world."[1] Optics provides a vocabulary essential to Proust's thematic development. Not only does optics illuminate the external world, values, and development of the action, communicating these to the reader with a consistent vocabulary, it also illuminates the inner world of the self: "Sleep, memory, imagination, sense of identity—here are indeed the basic areas of refraction and illusion, and Proust allows his optical imagery to crystallize around these crucial mental operations" (12). The optical imagery in *A la recherche du temps perdu* also affects the reader, allowing him to experience a sort of relativity resulting from the different perspectives of memory. These perspectives cause a change from a spatial to a temporal depth. As the normal subject-object relationship of reader to work dissolves, the work itself becomes a sort of optical instrument:

> Marcel withdraws into pure consciousness for the last fifteen pages [of *Le Temps retrouvé*], becomes a transparent subjectivity addressing itself to a work of art. This concluding self-effacement of Marcel as a person in any realistic or novelistic sense gives the book its quality of being less an object of our vision than an optical medium or instrument that modifies and directs our vision. (108)

In his work *Le Verre dans l'univers imaginaire de Proust,* David Mendelson supports the thesis that glass (and objects of glass) are the essential archetypes in Proust's work. Mendelson considers both Proust's scientific attitude and the more objective, or causal relations to the contemporary developments in glass.[2] The developments studied are in industry, science, and art. From art nouveau to aquariums, from the magic lantern to scientific instruments, Mendelson shows the modern developments, Proust's involvement with them, their particular manifestations in his work and, finally, how glass can be considered an essential structure of the work itself. This aspect of Proust's work has been discussed before, as the first defense offered against unfavorable criticism of Proust's translation of Ruskin:

> Most outstanding of its time for size and prominence, Sorel's article registers the first appreciation of Proust's new style: "Cet esthète pénétré ne traduit pas ses pensées en prose décadente. Il écrit quand il médite en rêve, un français flexible, flottant, enveloppant, en échappements infinis de couleurs et de nuances, mais toujours translucide, et qui fait songer, parfois, aux verreries où Gallé enferme ses lianes."[3]

Where Plantevignes sees glass, and Shattuck sees lenses, Beckett sees flowers and plants. To him these are the predominant images and they represent the human condition: "It is significant that the majority of [Proust's] images are botanical. He assimilates the human to the vegetal. He is conscious of humanity as flora, never as fauna."[4] The imagery here is as pervasive as those described by the two former critics. It describes Proust's "scientific" or "amoral" attitude toward people (which has upset more than one Proust critic): "This preoccupation accompanies very naturally his complete indifference to moral values and human justices. Flower and plant have no conscious will" (68). The state described here is similar to that which we shall see described by Schopenhauer, a sort of passive readiness, a "negative capability": "And, like members of the vegetable world, [Proust's characters] seem to solicit a pure subject, so that they may pass from a state of blind will to a state of representation" (69). As well as representing for Beckett the "subjective" or internal world, it suggests the state of the "objective" or external world: "When the subject is exempt from will the object is exempt from causality (Time and Space taken together). And this human vegetation is purified in the transcendental aperception that can capture the Model, the Idea, the Thing in itself" (69). Out of this passive, plant-like state of self and its reflected relativistic world the artist distills the essence of both in a united view of the world-all. Proust participates here in both the German Romantic tradition, becoming *eins mit dem Weltall,* and in the scientific tradition, probing the internal and external universe with a belief in a rationally verifiable order. As we shall see at the end of the following chapter (Proust's Scientific Spectacles), this meeting of mystical, or Eastern, and scientific, or Western thought, is one of Proust's more striking achievements.

Perhaps the most discussed of the scientific aspects is that of the importance of the medical sciences (in Proust's personal life, in his world view, and in the imagery, language, philosophy, subject matter, and structure of his work). In his work *L'Univers médical de Proust,* Serge Béhar states that: "L'œuvre de Proust est le seul exemple d'une intégration si large de la langue d'Hippocrate qui devient un élément du style littéraire."[5]

The critical reactions to this "univers médical" are varied. For Jean de Pierrefeu it is a nefarious intrusion. A member of the "classical" group of critics, Pierrefeu "declares that most of Proust's work is 'medical observation' which has no place in literature."[6] André Maurois takes a more positive approach, finding Proust's images "originelles et actuelles. Il ne craindra pas de les emprunter aux disciplines les plus diverses. Proust doit quelques-unes de ses plus belles images à la physiologie et à la pathologie."[7] For Béhar, this aspect is fundamental to understanding *A la recherche du temps perdu:* "Le roman est incompréhensible sans ce parallélisme entre le profil médical de Proust et celui de ses personnages" (219).

Among the different medical sciences, that of the newly emerging science of psychology is perhaps the most important, and the most discussed. In the early years of Proust criticism some of the best apologies of his work were in the classical vein. With the publication of *Sodome et Gomorrhe II* (1922), he is described as a "moralist and a psychologist," with a number of important studies on the latter aspect appearing at this time. Even earlier (1913-14), G. de Pawlowski "remarks that apparently literary formulae are changing and that the old rudimentary psychology of the traditional French novel is yielding to a sort of 'bactériologie psychologique.' "[8] The old division of science and literature into two distinct disciplines is dissolving.

Some critics see Proust as an isolated phenomenon. Jean Carrère describes Proust "comme un phénomène n'ayant rien en commun avec son temps."[9] For others he is a first, an original in this merging of fields:

"C'est la première fois que les différents étages de la conscience sont représentés à nos yeux d'une manière sensible, la première fois qu'on nous montre à nous-mêmes que nous ne vivons pas sur un seul plan, la première fois qu'on nous fait comprendre que chacun de nous est plusieurs."[10] From botany, with its implied objectivity and orderliness of observation, methodology, and classification, to psychology, where the object of study is now "plusieurs," as is the subject doing the observing, the problems of "scientific objectivity" and methodology become progressively more apparent. How can one study the self of another? And, even if one undertakes an auto-analysis, the problem of perspective, of a distortion of the self under study by the very act of observation remains. As shall be seen later, Proust is quite aware of this, and referred to it as his most difficult task. Nevertheless, it is with the detachment described earlier by Beckett that Proust attempts to observe man's internal world:

> Ce n'est peut-être pas la première fois dans l'histoire des sciences ou de la philosophie qu'un homme adopte une attitude aussi détachée à l'égard des phénomènes dont il est le sujet. Mais c'est certainement la première fois dans l'histoire de la littérature. Et même je crois que c'est la première fois dans l'histoire de toutes les disciplines humaines qu'elle est adoptée à l'égard des phénomènes de la conscience, avec une aussi complète et tranquille rigueur. (Rivière 51)

Literature and psychology share a common ground, the study of the internal, the unconscious workings of the self. Just how similar these two activities are we shall see in more detail with Louis Baudry's *Proust, Freud et l'autre*. As Elisabeth Czoniczer notes:

> Lorsque la psychologie devient comme une science complémentaire de la médecine, l'intérêt des écrivains s'étend sur elle. . . . Car, s'il y a des points de contact entre la médecine et la littérature, il y en a bien plus encore entre la littérature et la psychologie. L'objet d'étude de celle-ci fait aussi la préoccupation principale de toute littérature. . . . Les psychologues se rendent compte de tout ce que leurs études ont de commun avec le travail littéraire. Ils considèrent les écrivains presque comme des confrères dont leurs théories justifient souvent l'intuition, et ils les citent souvent. (27)

Though there is much discussion concerning what, if any, relationship there may have been between Proust's and Freud's views and their work, the opening of J. M. Charcot's clinic in Paris in 1880 appears to have played an important part in both their lives. Proust has also been compared to C. G. Jung, although somewhat less; here a very different sort of relationship requires a different sort of comparative technique. For the time being, however, let us simply note that Proust is not an isolated phenomenon: "Proust n'est pas un phénomène isolé: il est profondément enraciné dans son temps qui est le temps de son enfance et de sa jeunesse, qui est l'époque où le réalisme fait place au symbolisme" (Czoniczer 162).

Finally, before turning to a more detailed discussion of Proust's rootedness in the spirit of the time, we turn to Proust the physicist. His psychological observations concerning man's subjective, internal universe, combined with his observations concerning physical laws of the "objective," external universe suggest a very modern and unified view of "les deux infinis."

Briefly put, Proust's world-view was relativistic. In "The Glory of Motion" Claude Pichois shows how, even though Einstein's General Theory of Relativity was not widely known, the technological developments of the time were important enough to manifest themselves in contemporary literature, including *A la recherche du temps perdu:* "Si l'univers de Proust est un univers de la relativité et de l'instabilité—ce qui le rendit si étrange aux premiers lecteurs—, il le doit à une vitesse réelle ou à une vitesse potentielle. Cet univers porte une date."[11]

As with the physical certainties of time and space in the external world, the notion of an ordered, positivistic, fixed self also gives way to that of a more fragmented, relativistic plurality of selves. Parallels between Albert Einstein's universe of physical laws and that of Proust, itself made up of psychological laws, were made very early in the critical history of Proust's work. Critical repudiation of such parallels followed immediately and still continues. The mathematician Camille Vettard wrote a dedication in which he compared Proust and Einstein. The same Jacques Rivière who boldly compared Proust and Freud rejected the dedication on behalf of the *Nouvelle Revue Française.* Vettard wrote a defense, in which he referred to Proust's style:

> En s'ingéniant un peu, on pourrait dire que [la phrase-polype de Proust] est munie de multiples organes de préhension, parenthèses, incidentes et propositions subordonnées qui ne laissent rien perdre d'une

nombreuse conscience, de même que les systèmes de référence tentaculaires d'Einstein imposent leur prise à toutes les variations de courbure de l'univers.[12]

Vettard ends the defense calling "M. Proust un Einstein de la psychologie ou M. Einstein un Proust de la physique. . ." (131). In a letter to Vettard Proust tried to explain to him why Rivière rejected his dedication and, in so doing, once again showed his own pleasure at the comparison: "La raison, je ne sais s'il vous l'a dite, pour laquelle Rivière a hésité à publier, comme je lui avais demandé, votre dédicace, est . . . qu'il croyait me nuire en faisant présenter mon livre comme quelque chose d'abstrait, d'abstrus, surtout par la comparaison avec Einstein, ce qui est au contraire le plus immense honneur et le plus vif plaisir qu'on puisse me faire. . . ."[13]

It is as if Proust had taken Baudelaire's serpentine "soubressauts de la conscience" into the space-time continuum. The world Proust has created in his work reflects his own knowledge of both psychology and physics, the fundamental sciences in the effort to interpret nature and the psyche. It is not surprising, then, to find reflections in other thinkers of the time, each reflecting in his own discipline the world view of the other. Both Einstein and Proust have created worlds. Vettard speaks of Proust's style and psychology while George Painter makes another parallel:

> Algot Ruhe . . . wrote: "You accelerate and decelerate the rotation of the earth, you are greater than God". This, Proust himself felt, was going too far. "Even if he'd merely said I was as great as God," he objected . . . "it would still have been a bit much!" But the comparison with Einstein, if not with the Almighty, was attractive. *A la Recherche du Temps Perdu* was, indeed, the picture of a relativistic universe expanding and contracting in a curved space-time continuum; and when Benjamin Crémieux pointed out some apparent anachronisms in *Le Côté de Guermantes* Proust explained that these were due "to the flattened form my characters take owing to their rotation in time."[14]

As William Carter points out, while Proust's creation of a world is similar to that of Einstein's in its relativistic aspects, it also reflects the scientist's search for a Grand Unification Theory, or an underlying order which would tie together an otherwise fragmented and uncertain view of the world.[15]

Though not wishing to add to what Roger Shattuck refers to as the "irresponsible speculation which has attempted to associate Proust with Einstein and the principle of relativity" (43), we shall continue in as responsible a fashion as possible and do just that and, like Shattuck, go on to consider the relevance of Heisenberg's Uncertainty Principle to Proust's conception of the self, the world, and art. In an equally, if not more speculative vein, we shall apply the images and concepts developed in the preceding part of this work to Proust's vision of man's two worlds of nature and the psyche. In this way, we hope to arrive at the end of Proust's search for certainty in such a relativistic universe.

✦ ✦ ✦

II

Proust's Scientific Spectacles

THE FIRST INFLUENCE we shall discuss is that of the contemporary developments in glass, and the effect they had on Proust's world and the world of *A la recherche du temps perdu*. In the late nineteenth and early twentieth centuries progress in this field had its effects on architecture, electric lighting in the home, the microscope, the telescope and other ocular instruments. The importance of these developments is not lost on the writers of the time.

In architecture, glass and iron were signs of the times, an essential part of the style known as Art Nouveau. Proust makes numerous references to glass structures, such as the restaurant at the Grand Hôtel in Balbec. With its revolutionary use of iron and glass, the Grand Hôtel represents what is most modern in architectural developments for the time. "De fait, aux alentours de 1900, 'le fer et le verre dans l'architecture et la décoration sont un signe de modernisme.' "[1] It is clear that Proust was aware of these developments. Twice he refers to the work of Emile Gallé, one of the leading artists working with glass at the time. The first is at Balbec, in *A l'ombre des jeunes filles en fleurs*. Glass here serves to separate Marcel from the world. The images in the window could be a series of paintings, a sort of superimposed display of Monet's water lilies.

> ... dans le verre glauque et qu'elle boursouflait de ses vagues rondes, la mer, sertie entre les montants de fer de ma croisée comme dans les plombs d'un vitrail, effilochait sur toute la profonde bordure rocheuse de la baie des triangles empennés d'une immobile écume linéamentée avec la délicatesse d'une plume ou d'un duvet dessinés par Pisanello, et fixés par cet émail blanc, inaltérable et crémeux qui figure une couche de neige dans les verreries de Gallé. (1: 802)

In the second, much shorter, reference one can see the same elements—nature, a season, a moment captured in the glass of a window, and Marcel's isolation: "Bientôt l'hiver; au coin de la fenêtre, comme sur un verre de Gallé, une veine de neige durcie; et, même aux Champs-Elysées, au lieu des jeunes filles qu'on attend, rien que les moineaux tout seuls" (2: 392).

In a sense, it is through other objects of glass that Marcel tries to break out of the glass cage of his room. The magic lantern, for example, with its "verres grossissants" recreates little Marcel's bedroom. No longer is it an external light throwing an image on his window, it is an internal projection, recreating the wall. The image of the magic lantern is a dominant one throughout the work. It can be seen as a symbol of the working of the imagination of the artist, projecting his vision onto the world and thereby recreating it:

> . . . le narrateur recourt à la lanterne magique tout au long de sa recherche. Soulignons tout d'abord que l'image qui apparaît sur le mur n'est que la projection de celle qui s'inscrit dans l'un des verres de la lanterne. . . . De fait, les deux matières se fondent l'une dans l'autre: le réel forme l' "ossature" de l'imaginaire, par une opération de "transvertébration."
>
> N'est-ce pas au même résultat que voudrait parvenir le romancier? (Mendelson 102)

Two other developments in the glass industry also serve to help the narrator to explore the limits of the universe—from the smallest, using the microscope, to the most vast—using the telescope. The improvements in the quality of lenses played a great role in the expanding use of the microscope in the medical sciences, allowing increasingly precise observations in such fields as that of Proust's father, the epidemiologist Adrien Proust.

The same improvements added to the ability to make still larger and more regular lenses which helped to expand the astronomer's vision outward. The novelty, the expanse of such an ability is envied by the artists of the times:

> Rendons donc à cette matière l'hommage qui lui revient: "c'est bien le verre qui a rendu l'homme capable de porter ses regards à des profondeurs et des hauteurs si longtemps insoupçonnées, de les plonger— ou peu s'en faut—jusqu'au bacille le plus infime, de les élever— ou presque—jusqu'à la plus lointaine nébuleuse. "Les artistes

> contemporains de ces progrès de la science ne pouvaient que jalouser les savants qui plongeaient ainsi leur regard dans de nouveaux espaces, jamais perçus par la vision humaine. (Mendelson 38)

Proust's interest in astronomy was acknowledged at an early age. His family—already scientifically inclined by the presence of two doctors (Proust's father and brother)—was prone to encourage and indulge such pursuits. His microscopic vision is only equalled by his use of telescopic or astronomical view, as seen in *Le Temps retrouvé* where his particular, microcosmic descriptions are turned outward into an all-embracing, macrocosmic view of the universe (990-92, 1041).

Unlike the magic lantern, neither the telescope nor the microscope actually appear as part of the decor of the novel. They are used often as metaphors, however, and serve to symbolize the "Proustian vision," a search for an order, reaching from the most particular finite limits to the outermost limits of the visible universe, both extended by contemporary developments in the science of glassmaking. The microcosm reflects the macrocosm and the world in the lens of the microscope displays traits and reveals an order similar to those found in the lens of the telescope. No wonder then, that people should confuse the two. The narrator's apprehension concerning the reception of his work is founded on just this confusion of microscopic and telescopic views in time and space. He shows some of his novel to several acquaintances. No one understands anything.

> Même ceux qui furent favorables à ma perception des vérités que je voulais ensuite graver dans le temple, me félicitèrent de les avoir découvertes au "microscope," quand je m'étais au contraire servi d'un téléscope pour apercevoir des choses, très petites en effet, mais parce qu'elles étaient situées à une grande distance, et qui étaient chacune un monde. Là où je cherchais les grandes lois, on m'appelait fouilleur de détails. (3: 1041)

At the Guermantes' final party in *Le Temps retrouvé*, the narrator looks at the other members of the party "avec une satisfaction de zoologiste" (3: 944). He sees some people who appear not to have aged. But if one looks closer: "Mais si pour leur parler on se mettait tout près de la figure lisse de la peau et fine de contours, alors elle apparaissait tout autre, comme il arrive pour une surface végétale, une goutte d'eau, de sang, si on la place sous le microscope" (3: 945). A microscopic perspective in space, this provides the narrator with a telescopic view in time:

> C'était comme si on avait vu [les visages] à travers une vapeur colorante, un verre peint qui changeait l'aspect de leur figure mais surtout, par ce qu'il y ajoutait de trouble, montrait que ce qu'il nous permettait de voir "grandeur nature" était en réalité très loin de nous, dans un éloignement différent, il est vrai, de celui de l'espace, mais au fond duquel, comme d'un autre rivage, nous sentions qu'ils avaient autant de peine à nous reconnaître que nous eux. (3: 946-47)

In this comical confusion of time and space the microscopic aspect is carried even to the atomic level as Marcel is puzzled by one member of the party. He has finally gotten used to the idea that these old people really were his friends of many years ago, when he sees Odette's daughter, and mistakes her for the Odette he knew. He expresses his confusion:

> On part de l'idée que les gens sont restés les mêmes et on les trouve vieux. Mais une fois que l'idée dont on part est qu'ils sont vieux, on les retrouve, on ne les trouve pas si mal. Pour Odette ce n'était pas seulement cela; son aspect, une fois qu'on savait son âge et qu'on s'attendait à une vieille femme, semblait un défi plus miraculeux aux lois de la chronologie que la conservation du radium à celles de la nature. Elle, si je ne la reconnus pas d'abord, ce fut non parce qu'elle avait, mais parce qu'elle n'avait pas changé. (3: 948)

But has Marcel succeeded in breaking out of his glass confinement, is he any closer to the world than he was when observing it in the window? He is still limited to the contingencies of any subject-object relationship. In every case, the object is known only through (or as if through) a piece of glass—a window or a lens. The experience, the knowledge, however far-reaching, must therefore depend on the instrument of observation. This is not necessarily a negative conclusion, it is simply a phenomenological fact and it applies equally to the fundamental instruments of observation, our eyes. Any visual perception of an object depends on the transferral of its image (which depends on light, as it is carried to the eye on its waves or particles) to the lens of the eye, and is then transferred to the brain. Is it finally the object itself that is known, after its image travels across space and time, dependent on light for transportation and on the two retinas for receiving and delivery to the brain? The receiving and delivery begins with the innervation of the retina and, with the inverted image, an impression of depth is created by our binocular vision. Delivery to the brain is through a complicated interchanging of nerves between the left eye and the right brain, and the right eye and the left brain.[2] Interruptions, distortions, or even shut-downs may occur at any one of the points along the delivery—en route to the retina, on arrival, with its reception, or in the complex sorting on the way to the brain. And then there is the role of time. By the time the message sent is received, neither the origin nor the destination are the same. Both the sender and receiver are in movement. And, of course, the state of the whole "receiving apparatus"—the attention, or concentration, or awareness of the individual involved is of great importance. Each of these optical instruments, these complex synthesizers of visual information is custom-made. Every visual perception is founded on a subjective apparatus, making any data obtained not as objective as one might think. This fact is a fundamental one in the common misconception of "science" itself as a basis for certainty:

> The invention of the microscope or the telescope . . . will [only] disclose what was utterly unpredictable from the levels of perception that we could achieve before that discovery. . . . As a method of perception—and that is all science can claim to be—science, like all other methods of perception, is limited in its ability to collect the outward and visible signs of whatever may be truth.
> Science *probes;* it does not prove. (Bateson 32)

However increased the ability to collect visual data, however expanded the perspectival limits in space, there is always time, incessantly making obsolete the knowledge obtained:

> Ainsi ce n'est qu'après avoir reconnu, non sans tâtonnements, les erreurs d'optique du début qu'on pourrait arriver à la connaissance exacte d'un être si cette connaissance était possible. Mais elle ne l'est pas; car tandis que se rectifie la vision que nous avons de lui, lui-même, qui n'est pas un objectif inerte, change pour son compte, nous pensons le rattraper, il se déplace, et, croyant le voir enfin plus clairement, ce n'est que les images anciennes que nous en avions prises que nous avons réussi à éclaircir, mais qui ne le représentent plus. (Proust 1: 874)

This world view is not new: "Heraclitus, you know, says that everything moves on and that nothing is at rest; and, comparing existing things to the flow of a river, he says that you could not step into the same river twice."³

For some, love would seem to offer an escape from these confines, but for Proust it offers no union, no certainty, no escape. His ocular imagery illustrates again the essential relativity of any knowledge in the usual subject-object relationship: "La vie vous avait complaisamment révélé tout au long le roman de cette petite fille, vous avait prêté pour la voir un instrument d'optique puis un autre. . . . [C']est une leçon de relativisme dans l'appréciation d'un corps, d'une vie de femme. . . " (2: 362-63). This "lesson in relativism" that is love for Proust is a major source of confusion in Marcel's life. Far from providing any certainty, it disorients him to the point that he doubts the existence of any causality at all:

> Devant les pensées, les actions d'une femme que nous aimons, nous sommes aussi désorientés que le pouvaient être devant les phénomènes de la nature, les premiers physiciens (avant que la science fût constituée et eût mis un peu de lumière dans l'inconnu), ou pis encore, comme un être pour l'esprit de qui le principe de causalité existerait à peine, un être qui ne serait pas capable d'établir un lien entre un phénomène et un autre et devant qui le spectacle du monde serait incertain comme un rêve. Certes je m'efforçais de sortir de cette incohérence, de trouver des causes. (1: 586-87)

His objectivity having been placed in doubt, he tries to probe for the truth, using a pair of psychological binoculars, an effort that succeeds only in a slight appeasement of his suffering: "Je tâchais même d'être 'objectif'. . . . Je tâchais de trouver entre ces deux optiques également déformantes celle qui me donnerait la vision juste des choses; les calculs qu'il me fallait faire pour cela me distrayaient un peu de ma souffrance. . . " (1: 587).

Through every pair of eyes, then, a different universe is seen. Marcel's isolation is man's isolation. Each of us is trapped in his own world. Art, however, the projection of one individual's world view onto a canvas or a page, can help break through these confines. As style is to the writer, so color is to the painter. For each, it is a question, "non de technique mais de vision. Il est la révélation, qui serait impossible par des moyens directs et conscients, de la différence qualitative qu'il y a dans la façon dont nous apparaît le monde, différence qui, s'il n'y avait pas l'art, resterait le secret éternel de chacun" (3: 895).

Only art, then, can help us out of the confines of our individual worlds. Through it, one may share in another's universe. Through it, one may look into the internal world of the self—both one's own, and that of another: "Par l'art seulement nous pouvons sortir de nous, savoir ce que voit un autre de cet univers qui n'est pas le même que le nôtre, et dont les paysages nous seraient restés aussi inconnus que ceux qu'il peut y avoir dans la lune" (3: 895). In observing the self of another the work of art is like the emanation of light from a distant star, the star being the self of the artist who created the work:

> Grâce à l'art, au lieu de voir un seul monde, le nôtre, nous le voyons se multiplier, et, autant qu'il y a d'artistes originaux, autant nous avons de mondes à notre disposition, plus différents les uns des autres que ceux qui roulent dans l'infini et, bien des siècles après qu'est éteint le foyer dont il émanait, qu'il s'appelât Rembrandt ou Ver Meer, nous envoient encore leur rayon spécial. (3: 895-96)

In the observation of one's own self, it is more of an ocular instrument, with the same contingencies as the other instruments mentioned: "En réalité, chaque lecteur est, quand il lit, le propre lecteur de soi-même. L'ouvrage de l'écrivain n'est qu'une espèce d'instrument optique qu'il offre au lecteur afin de lui permettre de discerner ce que, sans ce livre, il n'eût peut-être pas vu en soi-même. . . " (3: 911). Again, however, this is not negative: ". . . l'auteur n'a pas à s'offenser, mais au contraire à laisser la plus grande liberté au lecteur en lui disant: 'Regardez vous-même si vous voyez mieux avec ce verre-ci, avec celui-là, avec cet autre' " (3: 911).

Still another glass object is taken out of Proust's world for use in that of *A la recherche du temps perdu*. The aquarium, like the other objects of glass, serves first as an instrument of observation, then as an image suggesting separation and confinement:

> Redécouverts vers 1850-1860 par les naturalistes désireux de reproduire en laboratoire les conditions de vie naturelle des poissons, des mollusques et des plantes aquatiques, les aquariums furent perfectionnés au point d'imiter à merveille leur milieu naturel . . . l'aquarium était bien

> l'un des plus fascinants des "petits mondes divers et clos" au Bois de Boulogne. (Mendelson 38-39)

The subject-object relationship is still that of observer and observed, and the image of the aquarium allows the narrator, like the scientists and their objects of study, to place the human species in a sort of laboratory-like atmosphere. The observer (the subject) is able to resolve the paradox of how to observe a closed world. As described earlier by Beckett, he is able to observe in a clinical, "objective" fashion. Human beings (the object of study) are allowed to continue in their natural routines, in their natural habitat, often unaware of any observers, as fish are unaware of people outside the aquarium (unless it is touched). Also, the object of study, human beings, has become just that—an object of study. The best example of this is, again, at Balbec. The large bay window of the restaurant offers Marcel his first view of many characters, including Albertine, Andrée, and Robert de Saint-Loup. Here Marcel is part of the enclosed world of the "aquarium" (though it might be argued that the writer referred to is the narrator himself). The alienation here is not that of an individual, but of social classes: the elite of the "aquarium," and the "others," the workers and the "petits bourgeois" outside the restaurant looking in. The effect is heightened with another contemporary development dependent on glass, electric lighting. It is an ironic passage:

> Et le soir . . . à l'hôtel où, les sources électriques faisant sourdre à flots la lumière dans la grande salle à manger, celle-ci devenait comme un immense et merveilleux aquarium devant la paroi de verre duquel la population ouvrière de Balbec, les pêcheurs et aussi les familles de petits bourgeois, invisibles dans l'ombre, s'écrasaient au vitrage pour apercevoir, lentement balancée dans des remous d'or, la vie luxueuse de ces gens, aussi extraordinaire pour les pauvres que celle de poissons et de mollusques étranges (une grande question sociale, de savoir si la paroi de verre protégera toujours le festin des bêtes merveilleuses et si les gens obscurs qui regardent avidement dans la nuit ne viendront pas les cueillir dans leur aquarium et les manger). (1: 681)

The perspective is that of a "fish-eye" view, with the observed observing the observer observing him:

> En attendant, peut-être parmi la foule arrêtée et confondue dans la nuit y avait-il quelque écrivain, quelque amateur d'ichtyologie humaine, qui, regardant les mâchoires de vieux monstres féminins se refermer sur un morceau de nourriture engloutie, se complaisait à classer ceux-ci par race, par caractères innés et aussi par ces caractères acquis qui font qu'une vieille dame serbe dont l'appendice buccal est d'un grand poisson de mer, parce que depuis son enfance elle vit dans les eaux douces du faubourg Saint-Germain, mange la salade comme une La Rochefoucauld. (1: 681)

Certainly visions such as this must have offered Proust cause for some of his "fous-rires," which he was known to break into at unexpected moments. Besides the humor, one can see an image of a perspective to the infinite, of a world inside a world or, perhaps better said, of the little fish getting eaten by the bigger fish, which in turn is eaten by an even larger fish, and so on, lying in this "grande question sociale." One can also see a suggestion (albeit humorous) of the question of evolution here—the Darwinian and Lamarckian debate over acquired and inherited characteristics. This aspect and the question of scientific perspective will be discussed later.

Proust uses the aquarium again as an image for the Baron de Charlus's lifestyle, again to emphasize separation, here not so much of a socio-economic nature, but of sexual orientation. Charlus is as much in touch with the opinions of the other members of the Verdurin clan concerning himself as a fish is aware of people observing it in an aquarium:

> Ainsi M. de Charlus vivait dupé comme le poisson qui croit que l'eau où il nage s'étend au-delà du verre de son aquarium qui lui en présente le reflet, tandis qu'il ne voit pas à côté de lui, dans l'ombre, le promeneur amusé qui suit ses ébats ou le pisciculteur tout-puissant qui, au moment imprévu et fatal, . . . le tirera sans pitié du milieu où il aimait vivre pour le rejeter dans un autre. (2: 1049)

Thus the aquarium points out one difference between the narrator and the Baron. The former, with his multiple perspectives, is conscious of his situation and can draw a comic conclusion. Charlus, however, is unaware of his precarious position in the Verdurin clan, or aquarium, and can only be pitied.

Marcel's grandmother sees all this in a broader perspective. Using another image of confinement (though not one of glass) she compares the confined, snobbish worlds of the Verdurin clan and the Guermantes to a public bathroom. The attendant, "La Marquise," only lets a certain clientele use her facilities: "Et puis, dit-elle, je choisis mes clients, je ne reçois pas tout le monde dans ce que j'appelle mes salons" (2: 310). As they are leaving, Marcel's grandmother makes the rather sarcastic and socially levelling comment: "C'était on ne peut plus Guermantes et petit noyau Verdurin" (2: 312).

In another of the "petits mondes divers et clos" we find Marcel looking for his friend Robert de Saint-Loup in a private room of a restaurant. In direct contrast to "La Marquise's" "Cabinets," it offers an illuminating look into a private affair which, with the aid of mirrors and electric lighting, reflects an ugly image of an effort to escape the feelings of confinement and solitude through alcohol. The self has become the other. The effect is one of a perspective to the infinite:

> Le cabinet où se trouvait Saint-Loup était petit, mais la glace unique qui le décorait était de telle sorte qu'elle semblait en réfléchir une trentaine d'autres, le long d'une perspective infinie; et l'ampoule électrique placée au sommet du cadre devait le soir, quand elle était allumée, suivie de la procession d'une trentaine de reflets pareils à elle-même, donner au buveur, même solitaire, l'idée que l'espace autour de lui se multipliait en même temps que ses sensations exaltées par l'ivresse et qu'enfermé seul dans ce petit réduit, il régnait pourtant sur quelque chose de bien plus étendu en sa courbe indéfinie et lumineuse, qu'une allée du "Jardin de Paris." (2: 171)

Marcel looks at a reflection of his inebriated state and smiles at it. As Mendelson notes (167), this smile will disappear as Marcel enters the hell of "Sodome et Gomorrhe." According to Beckett, Proust observes as a botanist would. Or as Maurois writes, "quand il observe les manifestations du désir, Proust le fait en naturaliste" (236). This same scientific interest ("même curiosité psychologique, même désir et besoin naturel d'observation" [Plantevignes 30]) leads the narrator from observation to observation, ever more penetrating, ever more carefully positioned in an observation post so as not to disturb the object of observation. In other words, the narrator is a voyeur. To George Painter's mind Proust is one as well:

> The Narrator's three crucial revelations of sexual deviation are all associated with spying—not, like Stendhal in the scabrous engraving,

> through a keyhole, but by a characteristically Proustian symbol through a window. He becomes aware of Lesbianism by watching Mlle Vinteuil and her friend through the window at Montjouvain, of sodomy when he sees the meeting of Charlus and Jupien in the Duchesse's courtyard, and of solitary pleasure in the upstairs lavatory at Combray, where the Narrator himself is detected from outside by the flowering currant and the castle-keep of Roussainville. All these are probably based on real memories.... (2: 120)

In line with his labelling of the narrator's "solitary pleasure" as a "sexual deviation," Painter seems reluctant to go too far with Proust, or the narrator, and he does not mention the final scene in Jupien's male brothel. He seems to ignore not only the importance, but the existence of the particular perspective offered by "the blind" afforded by a keyhole or a peep-hole. Less reluctant, Howard Moss traces the focusing of vision to the peephole, into the depths of the hell of Jupien's male brothel: ". . . the bedroom window at Combray becomes a repetitive motif. It narrows into a 'peep-hole' behind which a once imagined, and now desired and detested action takes place, transforming the childhood pictures of legend and history projected by Marcel's magic lantern into a horrifying vision of sexual love."[4] It is worth noting that it is at Jupien's brothel that the narrator's (and reader's) vision is focused onto the small "croix de guerre" left at the house (3: 820) and revealed later by Françoise (3: 841) as belonging to Robert de Saint-Loup. Not surprisingly, this particular bit of knowledge results in a change in the narrator's perspective with regard to all the "data" collected on this particular human "specimen."

Though ocular imagery is used to describe love in general, homosexuality is at the center of these "voyeuristic" experiences. Proust appears to be associating these ocular images with the homosexual—an allegory for his attempts to probe both into the dark, hidden places of the psyche, and to take his clinical observations into the darkest "closets" of human activity. As the author's friend, Marcel Plantevignes wrote of Proust:

> Je crois avoir déjà dit que Proust, dans son extrême curiosité des réalités psychologiques humaines recherchait jusqu'aux perversités et lorsqu'il les rencontrait s'attardait dans leur étude. Ce n'était pas curiosité malsaine, mais seulement désir d'explorateur, de découvrir toujours plus loin la mentalité humaine, même dans ses déformations, et appétit de connaître du chirurgien au scapel descriptif de psychologue. (460)

The association works especially well in French, with the word "inversion" referring both to the ocular occurrence and to homosexuality. Referring to the scene at the restaurant with Saint-Loup, Mendelson writes: "Il nous semble ici que Proust, fort curieusement, discerne une certaine homologie entre les lois de l'inversion et les lois de l'optique . . . " (167). J. E. Rivers also discusses the "structural inversion" of Proust's technique, giving an interesting list of inversions found in Proust's novel.[5]

We shall return to this theme later, both in the section concerning natural history and in the summary of Proust's scientific perspectives. It is interesting to note before continuing, however, the similarity between the inverted imagery seen here as a major perspective in Proust's world view and that described by Thomas Kuhn to explain his theory of scientific revolutions and paradigms. In a chapter entitled "Revolutions as Changes of World View," Kuhn writes: "Rather than being an interpreter, the scientist who embraces a new paradigm is like the man wearing inverting lenses. Confronting the same constellation of objects as before and knowing that he does so, he nevertheless finds them transformed through and through in many of their details."[6]

The last ocular instrument to be discussed in this chapter does not belong in the realm of science. The kaleidoscope is, in fact, the very antithesis of the common conception of a "scientific" instrument—cold, objective, precise, analytical. The kaleidoscope is a toy. It is a plaything with no practical purpose, amusing children and adults from the nineteenth century to the present day. Its "peephole" into "un des petits mondes divers et clos" has fascinated many (resulting in the loss of many kaleidoscopes to inquiring hands). At the twist of a hand, a whole new order, a whole new world is created. It is not surprising that Proust used it as a very striking image of his own world view, ever turning in the space-time continuum.

Like the telescope, the microscope, the binoculars and the aquarium, it is never a part of the decor of Marcel's world as is the window, or the magic lantern. It is unlike any of the other ocular images discussed so far in that it depends on nothing external to the instrument except light. It holds its own object of observation, not even requiring a blank wall for it to project its image on. A perfect escape for the confined, the solitary, the uncertain Marcel. A perfect metaphor for a vision of a world in motion. The image appears early, in the third paragraph of *Du côté de chez Swann*. It is used to suggest the narrator's semi-conscious state, one part awake, one part asleep. It is interesting to note that light—the only thing the kaleidoscope depends on—is absent. It is the light of consciousness that will try to fix this world in motion, and it is the objective world that has fallen asleep (not unlike in the passage with the steeples of Martinville and Vieuxvicq, where it seemed it was they who were in motion and not Marcel, speeding along in the carriage with Dr. Percepied):

> Je me rendormais, et parfois je n'avais plus que de courts réveils d'un instant, le temps d'entendre les craquements organiques des boiseries, d'ouvrir les yeux pour fixer le kaléidoscope de l'obscurité, de goûter grâce à une lueur momentanée de conscience le sommeil où étaient plongés les meubles, la chambre, le tout dont je n'étais qu'une petite partie et à l'insensibilité duquel je retournais vite m'unir. (1: 4)

As with the other instruments, it is applied also to society: "Mais pareille aux kaléidoscopes qui tournent de temps en temps, la société place successivement de façon différente des éléments qu'on avait crus immuables et compose une autre figure. . . . Ces dispositions nouvelles du kaléidoscope sont produites par ce qu'un philosophe appellerait un changement de critère." Speaking of the Dreyfus affair, the narrator writes: "L'affaire Dreyfus en amena un nouveau, à une époque un peu postérieure à celle où je commençais à aller chez Mme Swann, et le kaléidoscope renversa une fois de plus ses petits losanges colorés." All these changes, he comments, do not keep people from thinking there will be no more changes, any time the world seems immobile, "de même qu'ayant vu commencer le téléphone, ils ne veulent pas croire à l'aéroplane" (1: 517).

The kaleidoscope, then, provides an image for the individual's relationship to a society and a world in flux. It also suggests Proust's notions of love and the contrast between the eternal verities of art and the ethereal judgements of the critical world. With the former, the kaleidoscope recalls the "kaléidoscope de l'obscurité." Now, Marcel is not only confused with regard to the nature of the things around him, he is in pain due to uncertainty with regard to people. Balbec has turned into "une vue de l'Enfer": "Nous croyons savoir exactement les choses, et ce que pensent les gens, pour la simple raison que nous ne nous en soucions pas. Mais dès que nous avons le désir de savoir, comme a le jaloux, alors c'est un vertigineux kaléidoscope où nous ne distinguons plus rien" (3: 519).

Recalling the telescopic image of art mentioned earlier, where it allows one to see into others' worlds, and which is the result not of intelligence, but of vision, Proust criticizes the critics and defers to the "instinct" of the public, despite its many imperfections:

> Mais dès que l'intelligence raisonneuse veut se mettre à juger des œuvres d'art, il n'y a plus rien de fixe, de certain: on peut démontrer tout ce qu'on veut. . . . Car il y a plus d'analogie entre la vie instinctive du public et le talent d'un grand écrivain, qui n'est qu'un instinct religieusement écouté au milieu du silence imposé à tout le reste, un instinct perfectionné et compris, qu'avec le verbiage superficiel et les critères changeants des juges attitrés. Leur logomachie se renouvelle de dix ans en dix ans (car le kaléidoscope n'est pas composé seulement par les groupes mondains, mais par les idées sociales, politiques, religieuses, qui prennent une ampleur momentanée grâce à leurs réfraction dans des masses étendues. . .). (3: 893-94)

Telescopes, microscopes, magic lanterns, windows, aquariums and kaleidoscopes. All instruments of glass, and all undergoing fundamental changes in Proust's time. Evidence of Proust's interest in and knowledge of each is abundant, as is that of their importance in *A la recherche du temps perdu*. Each serves first as an instrument of observation, probing ever farther into space—both micro- and macrocosmic. Proust utilizes each of the objects to observe not only in space, but also in time. He uses the images of the instruments to describe his research not only into nature, but also into the human psyche. While nearly all can be said to be "scientific"—involved in the rational, conscious, orderly collection through objective observation of classifiable data referring to a fixed world—they consistently point out the limits of such perceptual knowledge. As Roger Shattuck writes: "This rational construction of space was not to be systematically broken down until the nineteenth century, when an optical revolution of new instruments and new theories of color and light provided expressive technique for the restlessness of modern sensibility" (145). Each instrument, while allowing closer observation, only serves to illuminate the narrator's isolation and confinement. Only in art can they be escaped, and only in an art based on the antithesis of scientific activity, intuition. West meets East: "And the Oriental aspect of *A la recherche* goes very deep. . . . One of the greatest achievements in the Western tradition of the novel, *A la recherche* also joins the Oriental tradition of works of meditation and initiation into the mysteries of life. We can read as far into it as our age and understanding allow" (Shattuck 119). The scientist Proust and the artist Proust, both exploring the worlds of nature and the psyche, is searching for laws, for order, for certainty. How better to begin the expression of his vision of the world than with optical theory?

✦ ✦ ✦

III

Proust in Motion

LIKE PROUST, THE NARRATOR is known for his sedentary existence, confined to his room or moving in the closed world of the salons. He does get up and around, however, at times picking up enough speed to experience the unsettling feeling of a world in motion. No longer is one anchored in a stable universe based on rational, causal principles. The Cartesian and Newtonian mechanical universe, open to rational, conscious observation, is left behind for an Einsteinian universe, in which space is confounded with time, causality is replaced by statistical probability, and conscious, rational observation no longer necessarily precedes theory formation in the search for truth. The narrator can be said to have travelled down Heraclitus's river into Einsteinian eddies in the space-time continuum.

The succession of the narrator's experiences is a mirror image of those of Marcel's Aunt Léonie—the former (until the end of the work) knowing increasing mobility in a movement outward—the latter, increasing immobility in an inward movement: "... cette tante Léonie ... n'avait plus voulu quitter, d'abord Combray, puis à Combray sa maison, puis sa chambre, puis son lit et ne 'descendait' plus, toujours couchée dans un état incertain de chagrin, de débilité physique, de maladie, d'idée fixe et de dévotion" (1: 49). Her state of inertia has led her to a state of complete uncertainty as to the objective validity of the information brought to her by her senses. Both the origin of the information and the possibility of its objective verification by another are in doubt:

> Dans la chambre voisine, j'entendais ma tante qui causait toute seule à mi-voix ... dans l'inertie absolue où elle vivait, elle prêtait à ses moindres sensations une importance extraordinaire; elle les douait d'une motilité qui lui rendait difficile de les garder pour elle, et à défaut de

> confident à qui les communiquer, elle se les annonçait à elle-même, en un perpétuel monologue qui était sa seule forme d'activité. (1: 50)

Like Aunt Léonie, the narrator is confined to his room at the beginning of the novel. Marcel's movement outward begins with the experience of the exile of his bedroom. First he is on the stairs, then in the living room, then walking through the two ways of Combray, then riding (on horses, in carriages, automobiles and trains). Like memory, travel is fundamental to an understanding of Proust's work. As with memory, inertia is broken. The laws of time and space destroyed, and a new law, a new order, a new certainty are created. As Georges Poulet writes: "On ne saurait donc assez insister sur le caractère surprenant, et même véritablement inouï, du voyage, dans l'œuvre proustienne. Car il rompt une loi; il enfreint une règle qui, chez Proust, a une sphère d'application littéralement universelle; et, de ce fait, il change l'aspect de l'univers. Le voyage bouleverse l'apparence des choses."[1] Travelling takes Marcel out of his confinement, his isolation. Novelty replaces habit. Things and places—heretofore separated into little "closed vases"—are reunited. Space itself undergoes a sort of metamorphosis. As memory brings together events isolated in time, so travel—equally as magically—brings together places and people isolated in space. In both cases—in the internal, subjective travel of memory in time, and in physical travel in space—he is able to escape the paralysing inertia and uncertainty experienced by his Aunt Léonie. His "least sensations" are no longer experienced in isolation. Marcel finds them instead in the outside world, endowing them with an objective validity. Paradoxically, according to Poulet, the unsettling experience of travelling provides him with a new certainty, a new order, a new sort of grace. The walls of his "diverse and enclosed worlds" fall—magically—even supernaturally:

> L'expérience du voyage est aussi inexplicable chez Proust que l'expérience du souvenir. Inespérée, impréparée et explicitement contraire à toute expérience antécédente, elle surgit tout à coup, comme une grâce céleste, pour sauver l'être qui l'éprouve, sinon du désespoir, au moins de la paralysie. Tout voyage, même sans tapis volant, est pour Proust une action magique. Magique, ou, si l'on veut, surnaturelle. (93-94)

Before considering these voyages, we shall look first at other means of transport, other means of escape from his confinement, none of which require physical movement in space.

1. Immobile Means of Transportation

Reading is the first of these immobile means of transport. The narrator can slip out of his world and into the world of the work he is reading. He even leaves his own self, becoming the protagonist ("il me semblait que j'étais ce dont parlait l'ouvrage" [1: 3]). The chair he reads (and falls asleep) in becomes a magic chair: "le fauteuil magique le fera voyager à toute vitesse dans le temps et dans l'espace" (1: 5). Sleep, the nightly (or for Proust, daily) vertical voyage into the unconscious is the second immobile means of escape. It is compared by the narrator to travelling in an automobile, a train, and an airplane. Marcel interrupts Aunt Léonie's sleep. This results in a sort of shifting of gears: "J'allais m'en aller doucement, mais sans doute le bruit que j'avais fait était intervenu dans son sommeil et en avait 'changé la vitesse', comme on dit pour les automobiles" (1: 109). Those uncertain moments of waking, already described as kaleidoscopic (1: 4), are also compared to the experience of stepping off a moving train:

> Pourtant dire ces paroles, au lieu de celles que continuait à penser le dormeur à peine éveillé que j'étais encore, me demandait le même effort d'équilibre qu'à quelqu'un qui, sautant d'un train en marche et courant un instant le long de la voie, réussit pourtant à ne pas tomber. Il court un instant parce que le milieu qu'il quitte était un milieu animé d'une grande vitesse, et très dissemblable du sol inerte auquel ses pieds ont quelque difficulté à se faire. (3: 122)

Nearly eight hundred pages later the image is transformed when the narrator writes of "le Rêve." In the voyage of sleep a past moment is transformed from an image of a pale, distant star (fixed in space, as the moment is supposedly fixed in time) to one of an airplane. The supposedly fixed star is in movement. A new meaning has been given to the notion of distance. Deceptively close to the magical voyage involved with the "plaisir spécial," the experience of sleep does not contain the necessary elements to bring Marcel the certainty for which he searches. From the distant stars of distant times to the approach of speeding airplanes, sleep supplies Marcel with an imagery for the internal world of the self which is similar to that used in his description of the sky in his apocalyptic experience in the darkest of nights at Jupien's male brothel in Paris during World War I:

> N'avais-je pas vu souvent en une nuit, en une minute d'une nuit, des temps bien lointains, relégués à ces distances énormes où nous ne

> pouvons plus rien distinguer des sentiments que nous y éprouvions, fondre à toute vitesse sur nous, nous aveuglant de leur clarté, comme s'ils avaient été des avions géants au lieu des pâles étoiles que nous croyions, nous faire revoir tout ce qu'ils avaient contenu pour nous, nous donnant l'émotion, le choc, la clarté de leur voisinage immédiat,—qui ont repris, une fois qu'on est réveillé, la distance qu'ils avaient miraculeusement franchie, jusqu'à nous faire croire, à tort d'ailleurs, qu'ils étaient un des modes pour retrouver le Temps perdu. (3: 912)

Sleep takes one on a trip not only in time and space, but also from self. Memory—of time, place, and self—can serve as a "secours d'en haut" to help pull Marcel out of "la mer d'irréel qui [le] baignait encore" (3: 123). As we have seen, as the ability to orient oneself in time and space may be distorted, so this effort of consciousness, of voluntary memory may be one founded not on a solid, causal reality, but one based more on something akin to the laws of chance:

> Et souvent une heure de sommeil de trop est une attaque de paralysie après laquelle il faut retrouver l'usage de ses membres, rapprendre à parler. La volonté n'y réussirait pas. . . . On a souvent près de soi, dans ces premières minutes où l'on se laisse glisser au réveil, une variété de réalités diverses où l'on croit pouvoir choisir comme dans un jeu de cartes. . . . (3: 123)

This uncertainty with regard to one's self, despite the efforts to orient oneself in the supposedly fixed, familiar, external world, and in an internal world based on memories of the same is particularly evident, then, in these waking moments. Everything is in movement. The uncertainty experienced is a fundamental one, reminiscent of the transitory nature of our existence:

> Mais le plus souvent, angoisse—angoisse de voir la mobilité déjà si effrayante en elle-même, de notre être. Car comment ne pas perdre de sa foi en la vie, quand on s'aperçoit que la seule fixité qu'on y croyait trouver—fixité des lieux, fixité des objets qui y sont situés—est illusoire? La mobilité des lieux nous enlève notre dernier recours. Elle nous désancre. A quoi pouvoir se raccrocher, si, comme les temps et comme les êtres, les lieux aussi sont emportés dans cette course qui ne mène qu'à la mort? (Poulet 20)

A similar experience is described in one of the narrator's (and Proust's) favorite books, *Mille et une Nuits.* "L'histoire du dormeur éveillé" is specifically mentioned in *A l'ombre des jeunes filles en fleurs* when Marcel, eating some cakes served on a plate, is reminded of his aunt's china at Combray: "Ils me rappelaient ces assiettes à petits fours, des *Mille et une Nuits,* qui distrayaient tant de leurs 'sujets' ma tante Léonie quand Françoise lui apportait, un jour, 'Aladin ou la Lampe Merveilleuse', un autre, 'Ali-Baba, le Dormeur éveillé' ... " (1: 904). Like Marcel, Abou Hassan, the protagonist of the story, is "A la recherche du temps perdu." A look at the first page of the story provides an interesting alternate interpretation to the title of Proust's work. Abou is a young man, in his thirties, who has been a good son all of his life. His father dies, leaving a substantial inheritance. One half he puts away. The other half he uses to make up for time lost in his prudent adolescence. In this story the Calif Haroun-Al-Raschid leaves the palace for one of his nocturnal trips into the city. Disguised as a merchant, the calif hopes to learn the undistorted truth of what is happening in the city, without letting anyone know it is the calif who is wandering, observing. It is interesting that Proust provides both the narrator and Charlus with the calif's reasons for their nocturnal prowling. In the latter one can see a justification of Howard Moss's earlier comment referring to the legendary, mystical world of the magic lantern turning eventually into a stranger sort of vision:

> Si je reviens sur la question du conducteur de tramway, reprit M. de Charlus avec ténacité, c'est qu'en dehors de tout, cela pourrait présenter quelque intérêt pour le retour. Il m'arrive en effet, comme le calife qui parcourait Bagdad pris pour un simple marchand, de condescendre à suivre quelque curieuse petite personne dont la silhouette m'aura amusé. (2: 610)

Abou parties away the second half of his inheritance. The result is a uniquely Proustian alienation: "La grosse somme qu'il avait consacrée à cette prodigalité et l'année finirent ensemble. Dès qu'il eut cessé de tenir table, ses amis disparurent."[2] Abou decides to have nothing more to do with anyone, but decides finally to invite a stranger—for one night only—to drink, dine, and converse with him. He meets the calif, they spend an evening together, Abou tells his story, expressing at the same time his wish to be calif for a day. The calif likes Abou, and allows him to realize his desire. He drugs him and takes him to the palace, ordering his servants to treat Abou as if he were the calif. Abou wakes, confused at the unfamiliar sight of all the fine things: "A ces objets si éclatants, Abou Hassan fut dans un étonnement et dans une confusion inexprimables. Il les regardait tous comme dans un songe: songe si véritable à son égard qu'il désirait que ce n'en fût pas un" (2: 439). After an initial acceptance of his new identity, Abou finally decides that he is still dreaming: " 'Bon! disait-il en lui-même, me voilà calife; mais ajoutait-il un peu après en se reprenant, il ne faut pas que je me trompe, c'est un songe, effet du souhait dont je m'entretenais tantôt avec mon hôte.' Et il refermait les yeux comme pour dormir" (2: 439). The unfamiliarity, the uncertainty one sees here we have encountered often in Proust's work. The unreliability of the sort of memory under discussion here (that is, a willed, conscious effort to orient oneself) is also experienced by the narrator. However, in one of those moments where involuntary memory exerts its power, erupting like a genie from a bottle, the world is transformed, the glass cage broken, and a certainty, a foundation on which to build an edifice emerges. In the following passage, the narrator, listening to a concert, is lost in time and space until he hears "la petite phrase":

> Où le situer? Dans l'œuvre de quel auteur étais-je? J'aurais bien voulu le savoir, et, n'ayant près de moi personne à qui le demander, aurais bien voulu être un personnage de ces *Mille et une Nuits* que je relisais sans cesse et où, dans les moments d'incertitude, surgit soudain un génie ou une adolescente d'une ravissante beauté, invisible pour les autres, mais non pour le héros embarrassé, à qui elle révèle exactement ce qu'il désire savoir. Or à ce moment, je fus précisément favorisé d'une telle apparition magique . . . plus merveilleuse qu'une adolescente, la petite phrase . . . vint à moi, reconnaissable sous ces parures nouvelles. (3: 249)

Though it may provide a chance to travel without moving, and though it may serve to reorient oneself (with limits and possibility of error) in space, time, and self, voluntary memory can offer no certainty. Involuntary memory, with its "special pleasure" (founded on a sensory contact with a particular of reality) offers the same advantage of travel without movement, with a foundation for certainty which lies outside the confines and limitations of time, space, and self. Paradoxically, this new certainty is preceded by an equally unsettling experience of uncertainty—a common theme in Proust's work. Memory sends the spirit on a voyage outside time and space. As Poulet writes: "La résurrection du passé, dit Proust en substance, force notre esprit à 'trébucher' entre les lieux lointains et les lieux présents 'dans l'étourdissement d'une incertitude pareille à celle qu'on éprouve parfois devant une vision ineffable au moment de s'endormir' " (18).

The references to *Mille et une Nuits* provide two other interesting facets which add a flavor of mystery and magic to Proust's work. First, they occur where there is some sort of displacement, a travelling by either an immobile or mobile means of transport. Second, the story to which he refers most often, "L'Histoire du dormeur éveillé," while full of mystery and adventure, contains no magic at all. It is an encounter with the calif which brings about the dramatic (and confusing) changes in Abou's life. (The coincidence itself might be hard to accept, but it does not rely on magic as such. In a sense, coincidence can be said to replace the role of magic. This is an important point, and we shall return to it later.) Perhaps the most 'mysterious' thing in this story is the brief mention of a door, the necessity of closing it, and the act of purposefully leaving it open. Abou asks the calif to be sure and shut the door when he leaves: "Ce que le calife lui promit d'exécuter fidèlement. . . . Le calife, suivi de l'esclave qui était chargé d'Abou Hassan, sortit de la maison, mais sans fermer la porte comme Abou Hassan l'en avait prié, et il le fit exprès" (2: 435-36). Abou blames the whole (mis)adventure on the calif's having left the door open. It is through the open door that the devil has entered Abou's house and, while he was sleeping, his dreams. That was the cause of his resultant confusion and (literal) torture, and when he finally admits this, he is free to return to his life as Abou Hassan. The calif has so craftily (and successfully) played on Abou's sense of reality that it offers him a way out, an explanation for both himself and others, and at the same time helps protect the secret of the calif's identity. He tells his mother that she has found the cause of his "mal":

> Je suis donc persuadé avec vous que le démon a trouvé la porte ouverte, qu'il est entré, et qu'il m'a mis toutes ces fantaisies dans la tête. Il faut qu'on ne sache pas à Mossoul d'où venait ce marchand, comme nous sommes bien convaincus à Bagdad que le démon vient causer tous ces songes fâcheux qui nous inquiètent la nuit quand on laisse les chambres où l'on couche ouvertes. (2: 461)

The themes of confinement and dreams must have had a strong appeal to Proust. Though it is an escape and not an intrusion that concerns Marcel when he is keeping Albertine in his apartment, one can hear an echo of this Oriental superstition. It is imperative that all windows and doors be kept shut, ostensibly for his health (Is the reference to the narrator of the stories that make up *Mille et une Nuits* merely coincidental?):

> Une fois Albertine sortie, je sentis quelle fatigue était pour moi cette présence perpétuelle, insatiable de mouvement et de vie, qui troublait mon sommeil par ses mouvements, me faisait vivre dans un refroidissement perpétuel par les portes qu'elle laissait ouvertes, me forçait—pour trouver des prétextes qui justifiassent de ne pas l'accompagner, sans pourtant paraître trop malade, et d'autre part pour la faire accompagner—à déployer chaque jour plus d'ingéniosité que Shéhérazade. (3: 131)

The sound of the opening of Albertine's window, is endowed with a power and meaning heretofore unknown: "Tout à coup, dans le silence de la nuit, je fus frappé par un bruit en apparence insignifiant, mais qui me remplit de terreur, le bruit de la fenêtre d'Albertine qui s'ouvrait violemment" (3: 402). After a rational consideration of the alternate interpretations as to the meaning of the sound, he decides that it is one of a wild, angry call of a bird flying to its freedom:

> Puis ce bruit avait été violent, presque mal élevé, comme si elle avait ouvert rouge de colère et disant: "Cette vie m'étouffe, tant pis, il me faut de l'air!" Je ne me dis pas exactement tout cela, mais je continuais à penser, comme à un présage plus mystérieux et plus funèbre qu'un cri de chouette, à ce bruit de la fenêtre qu'Albertine avait ouverte. (3: 402)

In the sound of the window opening Marcel can hear a presage of Albertine's final flight and ultimate death.

Like reading, sleep, and memory, drugs offer a magical means of immobile transportation in both Proust's world and the world of his novel. As an automobile can speed up or slow down, with the resulting alteration in the vision one has of the world passing by, so drugs may slow down or speed up the organism with an equally altered world view.

Due to his asthma, Proust started using drugs at an early age. By 1903 "Léon Daudet had declared: 'I can tell you, as a doctor, that Marcel Proust's ill-health is due to taking morphine.' "[3] Though Proust used drugs to both speed up and slow down, neither morphine nor alcohol nor cocaine seem to have been an overpowering threat. Of the first, Painter writes, "Proust undoubtedy took morphine occasionally at this time, with his parents' knowledge, but disliked it and never acquired the habit" (1: 320).

The same may be said for the latter two means of "transportation," as we shall see later.

Proust's insomnia, however, led him to take an array of somniferants later in his life. After the war, writes André Maurois, "Il prenait, pour dormir, jusqu'à un gramme cinquante de véronal par jour, ce qui le laissait, au réveil, assommé, presque asphasique, de quoi la caféine le réveillait, mais en le rapprochant de la mort."[4] Proust's need for coffee—hot, strong, and in great quantities—is well documented: "Car Proust saisissait au passage toutes les occasions de demander du café, et chaque fois n'en buvait pas moins de quatre tasses. . . ."[5] If an establishment's coffee was not strong enough, Proust would try to rectify the situation, as Marcel Plantevigne's recollection shows: "M. Le Rémois avait annoncé que selon et d'accord avec le conseil de M. Proust, il ferait désormais servir le café beaucoup plus fort à ses clients" (36). His inverted schedule getting the best of him, and finding it impossible to get to bed early enough to get some sleep before a (rare) outing with friends, Proust finally would simply not go to sleep. Coffee had also been prescribed to Proust for his maladies. Paul Morand recalls Proust's idea of the "mechanics" of a body:

> Et il m'initia à cette "mécanique" que tant de lettres et de confidences nous ont, depuis la mort de Proust, rendue familière; il appelait ainsi l'art de se conduire avec cette fameuse traîtresse qu'est la maladie, d'alterner les dosages savants (qui étonnaient bien les savants) des drogues, des excitants tempérés par des calmants, de la caféine corrigée par le bromure.
> —Vous mettez le pied à la fois sur le frein et sur l'accélérateur, lui fis-je observer.[6]

The narrator's relationship to other drugs is much the same. It is clear that the narrator argues from experience and, though he regards sleep as more powerful than a good dose of veronal, he knows the drug's possibilities: "J'ai toujours dit—et expérimenté—que le plus puissant des hypnotiques est le sommeil. Après avoir dormi profondément deux heures, s'être battu avec tant de géants, et avoir noué pour toujours tant d'amitiés, il est bien plus difficile de s'éveiller qu'après avoir pris plusieurs grammes de véronal" (2: 984). The effects of sleep are best known to those who know its absence. Its mysterious nature and its variety are appreciated most by someone who, normally using a drug to sleep, does not: "Il est aisé de parler de [la beauté] que crée l'opium. Mais pour un homme habitué à ne dormir qu'avec des drogues, une heure inattendue de sommeil naturel découvrira l'immensité matinale d'un paysage aussi mystérieux et plus frais" (3: 124). The narrator is an expert, a collector of various types of sleep. In changing the time or the place where he sleeps or in trying different drugs, the scientist is able to observe different types of sleep on his only possible subject, his own self. To this "gardener of dreams," the beauty he sees in variety is only surpassed by the beauty and strangeness of a sleep undistorted by the use of drugs:

> En faisant varier l'heure, l'endroit où on s'endort, en provoquant le sommeil d'une manière artificielle, ou au contraire en revenant pour un jour au sommeil—le plus étrange de tous pour quiconque a l'habitude de dormir avec des soporifiques—on arrive à obtenir des variétés de sommeil mille fois plus nombreuses que, jardinier, on n'obtiendrait de variétés d'œillets ou de roses. (3:124)

Drugs, then, can alter the speed of the mechanism of the individual, either with regard to the external world or the internal world, altering the speed of descent into (and resurrection from) the depths of the unconscious on the "chariot" of sleep. Again we see both Proust and the narrator here putting on the brakes, and there, accelerating their unmoving bodies.

Finally, before turning to Proust's mobile means of transportation, another innovation of the times must be considered. While it is, in a way, a means of avoiding movement (and, as such, is antithetical to the topic under discussion) the invention of the telephone resulted in a dramatic change in civilization, and Proust was aware of its importance. The telephone had a similar effect on Proust's world view as the other contemporary developments described in the previous chapter. It was a new instrument—magical, mystical—and shook the old, habitual, limiting notions of fixed time, space and self:

> Le téléphone n'était pas encore à cette époque d'un usage aussi courant qu'aujourd'hui. Et pourtant l'habitude met si peu de temps à dépouiller de leur mystère les forces sacrées avec lesquelles nous sommes en contact... l'admirable féerie à laquelle quelques instants suffisent pour qu'apparaisse près de nous, invisible mais présent, l'être à qui nous voulions parler et qui, restant à sa table, dans la ville qu'il habite (pour ma grand'mère c'était Paris), sous un ciel différent du nôtre, par un temps qui n'est pas forcément le même.... (2: 133)

Like a character from a magical tale, Marcel can accomplish his miracle with the "magic receiver" of the telephone. Magic, far from being opposed to technology, is once again to be found in the advances of science: "Et nous sommes comme le personnage du conte à qui une magicienne, sur le souhait qu'il en exprime, fait apparaître, dans une clarté surnaturelle, sa grand'mère ou sa fiancée . . . tout près du spectateur et pourtant très loin, à l'endroit même où elle se trouve réellement" (2: 133). For Eugène Nicole, "il est immédiatement évident que l'appareil n'est nullement traité [par Proust] comme objet technologique, mais que, par un renversement structurel, le code scientifique fait l'objet d'une sorte de régression dans l'ambiance de la féerie et dans l'imaginaire mythologique."[7] It is obviously with a sense of humor that Marcel waxes lyrical in his worship of the deities behind the magical apparatus. In this typically Proustian sentence Marcel refers to the telephone operators in a comical crescendo, rising first in a reverential tone, then adding an attitude of very down to earth aggravation with the powerful—yet real—telephone operators:

> Nous n'avons, pour que ce miracle s'accomplisse, qu'à approcher nos lèvres de la planchette magique et à appeler—quelquefois un peu trop longtemps, je le veux bien—les Vierges Vigilantes dont nous entendons chaque jour la voix sans jamais connaître le visage, et qui sont nos Anges gardiens dans les ténèbres vertigineuses dont elles surveillent jalousement les portes; les Toutes-Puissantes par qui les absents surgissent à notre côté, sans qu'il soit permis de les apercevoir; les Danaïdes de l'invisible qui sans cesse vident, remplissent, se transmettent les urnes des sons; les ironiques Furies qui, au moment que nous murmurions une confidence à une amie, avec l'espoir que personne ne nous entendait, nous crient cruellement: "J'écoute"; les servantes toujours irritées du Mystère, les ombrageuses prêtresses de l'Invisible, les Demoiselles du téléphone! (2: 133)

To have electricity and a telephone was a sign of being modern and of being part of the avant-garde. The Verdurins, of course, are among the first to have both. In contrast, some refused to enter into the mysteries watched over by the "Demoiselles du téléphone." Not surprisingly, Françoise is among these unbelievers, and refuses to have anything to do with this new invention (the narrator's crediting of Edison instead of Bell as the inventor of the telephone is less expected):

> Les progrès de la civilisation permettent à chacun de manifester des qualités insoupçonnées ou de nouveaux vices qui les rendent plus chers ou plus insupportables à leurs amis. C'est ainsi que la découverte d'Edison avait permis à Françoise d'acquérir un défaut de plus, qui était de se refuser, quelque utilité, quelque urgence qu'il y eût, à se servir du téléphone. (2: 730)

Because Françoise would not have answered the phone anyway, it is put in Marcel's room. Even there he fears missing Albertine's call, resulting in an immobility which forces Marcel back into a rapport with the world around him that reminds one of the opening scene of the novel (1: 8): "De peur de ne pas l'entendre, je ne bougeais pas. Mon immobilité était telle que, pour la première fois depuis des mois, je remarquai le tic-tac de la pendule" (2: 730).

As with the ocular images discussed in the preceding chapter, the telephone is first an instrument which helps Marcel break out of the confines of his cage. It is a sort of magical conducting wire, uniting people over time and space. For Marcel, it should be a welcome refinement of his system of communication with his grandmother at Balbec, where they tapped on the wall separating their adjacent rooms. On the contrary, due to the novel effect of hearing a disembodied voice, Marcel is forced to listen to it for the first time and to face—also for the first time—the very real effects of the passing of time on the person he cares the most about: "mais sa voix elle-même, je l'écoutais aujourd'hui pour la première fois . . . puis, l'ayant seule près de moi, vue sans le masque du visage, j'y remarquais, pour la première fois, les chagrins qui l'avaient fêlée au cours de la vie" (2: 134-35). Instead of uniting the two, the telephone only makes Marcel more aware of his separation and isolation: "Etait-ce d'ailleurs uniquement la voix qui, parce qu'elle était seule, me donnait cette impression nouvelle qui me déchirait? Non pas; mais plutôt que cet isolement de la voix était comme un symbole, une évocation, un effet direct d'un autre isolement, celui de ma grand'mère, pour la première fois séparée de moi" (2: 135).

2. Trains

By Proust's time the railway system had expanded, and had become a widespread means of transportation. While the fear of the railroad is evident in the writings of the Romantics, its incorporation into literature as a positive, dynamic, even magical force dates from the middle of the nineteenth century, as can be seen in an excerpt from a work by Paul de Kock, from 1842:

> ... voyager en chemin de fer ne fatigue pas; c'est un plaisir, un agrément ... on se sent rouler avec une douceur inconcevable, ou plutôt on ne se sent pas rouler. On voit fuir devant soi les arbres, les maisons, les villages ... tout cela passe! passe ... bien plus vite que dans une lanterne magique ... et tout cela est véritable, vous n'êtes point le jouet de l'optique! ... Le chemin de fer est la véritable lanterne magique de la nature.[8]

The question of perspective, the introduction of the notion of magic (in particular, the image of the magic lantern, and the optical uncertainty involved in the subject-object relationship), the consciousness of a fixed reality slipping away and the joy at experiencing it all remind one of Proust. Earlier in the century Gérard de Nerval had already used as many means of transportation as his epoch offered, including those of the immobile variety, all of which appear in his work. In 1832, Nerval endows the external world with mobility, and the passenger with immobility, an inversion which pervades Proust's description of the steeples (and which distinguishes it from anything in *Jean Santeuil*).

Roger Kempf is correct when he draws a parallel between the train and the elevator in Proust's novel: "... l'ascenseur et le chemin de fer sont tous deux attachés à une voie fixe, longue de tant de kilomètres ou d'étages, obéissant à l'horaire d'une compagnie ou à l'appel d'un supérieur."[9] Nonetheless, with the advent of the train, man's most elementary notions of time and space are shaken. Space is irrelevant. According to Benjamin Gastineau, only time is important: "Quelles transformations doivent maintenant s'effectuer dans nos manières de voir et de penser! Même les idées élémentaires du temps et de l'espace sont devenues chancelantes. Par les chemins de fer, l'espace est anéanti, et il ne nous reste plus que le temps" (Pichois 36). Space is a rational construct, a shadowy metaphysic: "La distance n'est plus qu'un être de raison, l'espace qu'une entité métaphysique dépourvue de toute réalité" (35). While we have not, of course, reached Einstein's time, these writers reflect a sense of the limits of the Cartesian, Newtonian, classical world view similar to that which we saw in the discussions concerning optical instruments and the telephone. With increasing efficacy in an empirical, rational, lawful world, our mechanical, solid reality becomes a magical creature, destroying our last certainties. The absolutism of classical thought, threatened from the eighteenth century by various notions of relativism, finally falls at the end of the nineteenth century. This is not lost on the French writers of the time.

The first "popular edition" of Einstein's theory came out in 1916 and, as the correspondence with Vettard shows, Proust was familiar with the physicist's views. It is evident that, by their time, both the scientist and the artist saw in the railroad train a vehicle universal enough to use as the expression of their relative world views. In his work *Relativity: The Special and the General Theory,* Einstein uses the train as a basis for his "clear explanation that anyone can understand." In the chapter "Space and Time in Classical Mechanics," Einstein first defines "the purpose of mechanics [which] is to describe how bodies change their position in space with 'time.' "[10] Not wishing to "sin against the sacred spirit of lucidity" he proceeds to explain his theory in terms of two men—one on a train, the other on the ground. He begins by questioning the notions of "position" and "space." If a stone is dropped from the moving train, "do the 'positions' traversed by the stone lie 'in reality' on a straight line or on a parabola? Moreover, what is meant here by motion 'in space' "(9)? His definitions of position and space, which he founded on classical, Euclidean geometry have eroded, the "rigid body" they depended on having become fluid, unfixed, the classical, mechanical world unhinged:

> Every description of events in space involves the use of a rigid body to which such events have to be referred. The resulting relationship takes for granted that the laws of Euclidean geometry hold for "distances," the "distance" being represented physically by means of the convention of two marks on a rigid body. . . . [Now, with regard to the train,] we entirely shun the vague word "space," of which, we must honestly acknowledge, we cannot form the slightest conception, and we replace it by "motion relative to a practically rigid body of reference." (8)

There is no causal connecting principle in Proust's world. A stereoscopic vision is evident in both time and space, and is of such a fundamental and universal nature as to be called by Poulet, paradoxically, "a general principle of discontinuity":

> La discontinuité temporelle est elle-même précédée, voire même commandée par une discontinuité plus radicale encore, celle de l'espace. Toutes deux s'entremêlent et s'aggravent mutuellement de façon si inextricable qu'il serait peut-être utile de faire ici quelques réflexions sur

> ce qui se trouve impliqué chez Proust par ce qu'on ne peut appeler autrement qu'un principe général de discontinuité. (55-56)

This principle is not limited to time and space, it applies also to the human condition and carries no certainty, no solid, unifying "help from above" in its universal manifestation. For Proust, distance is only a visible and tragic demonstration of the universal and inescapable impossibility of a happiness found in love. The subject in love is in one place, the object of love in another. The "little enclosed worlds" referred to earlier apply to people, moments and places alike. The principle of discontinuity, of separation, with its inherent lack of any causal connecting principle is universal. Yet, is there no connecting principle, no order, no certainty? As suggested earlier, coincidence may suggest such a "magical" or "mystical" reordering of the world. It is just such a chance occurrence that brings about Marcel's experience of the "special pleasure," as when he tastes the madeleine or sees the steeples of Martinville.

Einstein pursues the analogy of the train, adding conceptual problems in the form of varying points of reference, such as a flying raven and two events on the train viewed by someone on the embankment—are they simultaneous with reference to everyone? We have already seen difficulties in the simpler example, with one event and two perspectives, one of which is immobile. Now, the problem of a firm "truth," universal to all, with fixed references in space and time, is compounded by this problem of simultaneity.

One cannot help but imagine Proust's idea of the hopelessness of a certainty founded on the love of another, suggested by the description of love as a "lesson in relativism." In such a case, one does not even have the fixed referent of an embankment, as the "other" is in an equally mobile state. Both the subject, with its own multiplicity of selves, and the object of love, with its inherently uncertain and ever-changing and immobile nature, lead Marcel to experience the anguish of jealousy instead of the security of love. The development of his relationship with Albertine is, in essence, a description of this fundamental Proustian reality. Marcel is painfully aware that he can never truly know the "real" Albertine. Not only can he never find out exactly what happened, he cannot even escape the confines of his own temporal context. As Einstein explains, events which are simultaneous with reference to one coordinate system (such as on a train) are not simultaneous with regard to another coordinate system (such as on an embankment): "Every reference-body (co-ordinate system) has its own particular time; unless we are told the reference-body to which the statement of time refers, there is no meaning in a statement of the time of an event" (26). As we shall soon see, Marcel will try to imprison Albertine on the train, in the compartment, in his arms, and even there cannot do it. In the same passage, in the little Douville train we shall see what could be described as an artistic embodiment of Einstein's philosophical skeleton.

In *La Prisonnière* Proust uses the experience of stepping off a train to describe the equally unstabilizing experience of waking. In the first pages of *A la recherche du temps perdu,* it is the "sifflement des trains" in the middle of the night by which the narrator tries to orient himself in time and space. It is the novelty of the train ride which will later give him the certainty of memory: "et le petit chemin qu'il suit va être gravé dans son souvenir par l'excitation qu'il doit à des lieux nouveaux, à des actes inaccoutumés, à la causerie récente et aux adieux sous la lampe étrangère qui le suivent encore dans le silence de la nuit, à la douceur prochaine du retour" (1: 3-4).

In chapter three of *Sodome et Gomorrhe,* the narrator recalls a particular train trip along the coast of Normandy. The train offers Proust a chance to use another of the "petits mondes divers et clos"—the smallest being the compartment, then the corridor—with occasional interruptions by such stations as Doncières, Grattement, Maineville, etc., which seem more like images in a magic lantern show, offering topics of conversation, rather than a world with a reality external to that of the little world of the compartment. The passengers are no longer bound to the contingencies of an external reality. The spatial and temporal chain with the world outside the train has been broken:

> Une fois dans les voitures qui nous attendaient, on ne savait plus du tout où on se trouvait; les routes n'étaient pas éclairées; on reconnaissait au bruit plus fort des roues qu'on traversait un village, on se croyait arrivé, on se retrouvait en pleins champs, on entendait des cloches lointaines, on oubliait qu'on était en smoking, et on s'était presque assoupi quand, au bout de cette longue marge d'obscurité qui, à cause de la distance parcourue et des incidents caractéristiques de tout trajet en chemin de fer, semblait nous avoir portés jusqu'à une heure avancée de la nuit et presque à moitié chemin d'un retour vers Paris, tout à coup, après que le glissement de la voiture sur un sable plus fin avait décelé qu'on venait d'entrer dans le parc, explosaient, nous réintroduisant dans la vie mondaine, les éclatantes lumières du salon, puis de la salle à manger, où nous éprouvions un vif mouvement de recul en entendant sonner ces huit heures que nous croyions passées depuis longtemps,

> tandis que les services nombreux et les vins fins allaient se succéder autour des hommes en frac et des femmes à demi décolletées, en un dîner en ville et qu'entourait seulement, changeant par là son caractère, la double écharpe sombre et singulière qu'avaient tissée, détournées par cette utilisation mondaine de leur solennité première, les heures nocturnes, champêtres et marines de l'aller et du retour. (2: 1095-96)

Time, space, land, sea, darkness, light; all in one typically Proustian sentence—long, sinuous, unbroken except for minor punctuation—a seemingly fitting style to describe the experience of riding in a train.

If the restaurant of the hotel at Balbec was an aquarium for Proust, open to an icthyologist's inspection, the train is more of a social chemist's test-tube. The compartment is poorly lit, allowing Marcel to position himself in such a way that he can both imprison and take advantage of his proximity to Albertine: "... je m'arrangeais à être avec Albertine afin que mon amie ne pût être avec d'autres sans moi, et souvent pour une autre cause encore, qui est que nous pouvions tous deux faire bien des choses dans une voiture noire où les heurts de la descente nous excusaient ... d'être cramponnés l'un à l'autre" (2: 1096).

The social chemistry begins, heating up between Marcel and Albertine. It cools briefly as Marcel feels his chains to Albertine breaking by the experience of the freedom of travel (bringing to mind Charlus's inverted, immobile situation, dreaming of Venice, chained to the bed in Paris[11]). The train ride gives him "quelque impression de poésie," reawakening in him "le désir de faire des voyages, de mener une vie nouvelle, ... et même de rompre définitivement [leurs] relations, [ce qui lui] rendait aussi, et à cause même de leur nature contradictoire, cette rupture plus facile" (2: 1098).

A discussion of etymology provides the base for these acidic chemical undercurrents. Proust's biting humor is evident as Charlus joins the conversation between the pedant Brichot, the doctor Cottard, and the artist ("le sculpteur"). Charlus is obviously the object of Proust's acidic wit but so are the three representatives of their professions in the little world in the little train:

> Moi je demande l'explication de Thorpehomme, dit M. de Charlus. Je comprends "homme," ajouta-t-il, tandis que le sculpteur et Cottard échangeaient un regard d'intelligence. Mais Thorpe?— "Homme" ne signifie nullement ce que vous êtes naturellement porté à croire, baron, répondit Brichot, en regardant malicieusement Cottard et le sculpteur.

> "Homme" n'a rien à voir ici avec le sexe auquel je ne dois pas ma mère.
> "Homme" c'est "Holm," qui signifie "îlot," etc. (2: 1099-100)

Brichot's knowledge has the same effect on Charlus's "tendency" as it has on Marcel's sense of mystery in names; the former losing the sex, the latter, the flower (a correspondence which dominates *Sodome et Gomorrhe*). The "fleur" in such names as "Fiquefleur" and "Honfleur" does not suggest "flower," as Marcel had thought, but "port": "Déjà, avant les stations elles-mêmes, leurs noms . . . avaient perdu leur singularité depuis le soir où Brichot, à la prière d'Albertine, nous en avait plus complètement expliqué les étymologies" (2: 1098). In both cases the subjective projection onto the meaning of the word is lost, and the name of the place loses its particular significance. This is an especially disagreeable experience in Proust's eyes. A name is both an individual and a local thing. It is a name of a place, of a person, and a family. It is a "topological entity" resulting from its physical and its mental dimensions:

> Sous la forme d'un de ces phénomènes dont l'on use pour transporter les réalités objectives dans le monde mental, il est cette entité topologique inédite (issue de la fusion d'un site réel avec l'image d'une personne ou l'histoire d'une famille), qui est un lieu irréel, puisqu'il n'a pas sa place dans l'étendue externe, mais subjectivement réel, puisque situé dans les espaces de l'esprit. . . . (Poulet 46)

Another social (not to mention sexual—and comic) element is introduced at Doncières, where Robert de Saint-Loup is garrisoned and will often board the train with the other soldiers:

> —Mon Dieu, que de lieutenants vont essayer de monter! dit M. de Charlus, avec un effroi simulé. Je le dis pour vous, car moi cela ne me gêne pas, puisque je descends. —Vous entendez, docteur? dit Brichot. Le baron a peur que des officiers ne lui passent sur le corps. Et pourtant, ils sont dans leur rôle en se trouvant massés ici, car Doncières, c'est exactement Saint-Cyr, "Dominus Cyriacus." (2: 1100)

Despite Marcel's fragile claim of calm disinterest in the intrusions of Saint-Loup and his friends into his closed world, he is chained to Albertine by his jealousy. Saint-Loup enters and, despite the fact that Marcel believes Albertine to be a lesbian, he is forced to an even greater diligence in keeping her prisoner in this imperfect confinement of the train (and, inside the train, of the compartment):

> ... à Doncières, la brusque invasion d'un des charmants amis de Saint-Loup envoyé par lui (s'il n'était pas libre) pour me transmettre une invitation du capitaine de Borodino, du mess des officiers au Coq Hardi, ou des sous-officiers au Faisan Doré. Saint-Loup venait souvent lui-même, et pendant tout le temps qu'il était là, sans qu'on pût s'en apercevoir, je tenais Albertine prisonnière sous mon regard, d'ailleurs inutilement vigilant. (2: 1101-02)

Marcel, already submerged in the world of the compartment, is almost fished out by another friend, Bloch, who wants him to meet his father, who is waiting on the platform:

> Une fois pourtant j'interrompis ma garde. Comme il y avait un long arrêt, Bloch, nous ayant salués, se sauva presque aussitôt pour rejoindre son père, lequel venait d'hériter de son oncle et, ayant loué un château qui s'appelait la Commanderie, trouvait grand seigneur de ne circuler qu'en une chaise de poste, avec des postillons en livrée. Bloch me pria de l'accompagner jusqu'à la voiture. . . . Mais je souffrais trop de laisser Albertine dans le train avec Saint-Loup, ils auraient pu, pendant que j'avais le dos tourné, se parler, aller dans un autre wagon, se sourire, se toucher; mon regard adhérant à Albertine ne pouvait se détacher d'elle tant que Saint-Loup serait là. (2: 1101)

Marcel cannot be bothered, and this internal life and death struggle for Marcel is seen by Bloch as snobbery from his perspective on the platform while—given the description—from the reader's perspective it is the uncle who would appear to be the snob. Proust's opinion concerning love and jealousy is apparent in this passage, as is that concerning friendship. Marcel shows no concern for his two best friends, Robert de Saint-Loup and Bloch. Their respective social backgrounds—the first from the aristocracy, the second from the Jewish bourgeoisie—are irrelevant to Marcel. His little world has narrowed to the intense rapport formed between him and Albertine (suggesting another perspective to the infinite being a little world in the little world of the compartment, itself in the world of the little train). Whatever else may happen—including friendship—has the same relevance to his little world as the images of the countryside passing by in the window of the train have on the world of the compartment. The whistling of the train (in contrast to the "douceur prochaine du retour" it signifies at the very beginning of the work [1: 4]) suggests the transience and replaceability of friends: "Un autre [ami] serait à la gare suivante, si bien que le sifflet du petit train ne nous faisait quitter un ami que pour nous permettre d'en retrouver d'autres" (2: 1111).

The chemistry and the humor heat up, as Bloch is added to the compartment's mixture, causing a reaction in Charlus. Marcel recalls that Charlus had made an effort similar to the one he is currently making to get to know Bloch. His technique is to suggest that Marcel has not introduced him to Bloch out of a lack of respect for the baron: " 'Mais présentez-moi donc votre ami, ce que vous faites est un manque de respect pour moi,' et il avait causé avec Bloch, qui avait paru lui plaire extrêmement au point qu'il l'avait gratifié d'un 'j'espère vous revoir' " (2: 1101).

So we have Marcel keeping guard over Albertine, watching out for Saint-Loup while talking to Bloch, who has attracted the attention of Charlus, who is already the object of derision of the other members of the compartment. The social chemistry in this little world is agitated again as Charlus (representing the general dissimulation which, according to Proust, is at the base of any relationship) continues to try to use Marcel to get to Bloch. Charlus first tries asking Marcel a question concerning Bloch in "a tone so nonchalant, with an interest which seemed so simulated," that it would appear that he did not even bother to listen to the answers. He even makes it seem as if he is only asking questions out of politeness for Marcel. His efforts toward dissimulation, of course, do not fool the narrator: " 'Il a l'air intelligent, il a dit qu'il écrivait, a-t-il du talent?' . . . 'Il habite Balbec?' chantonna le baron, d'un air si peu questionneur qu'il est fâcheux que la langue française ne possède pas un signe autre que le point d'interrogation pour terminer ces phrases apparemment si peu interrogatives" (2: 1104).

The train, then, is a series of enclosed worlds, opening onto the external world at its different stops, as if they were worlds framed in a picture: "Un cadre de vie mondaine comme un autre, en somme, que ces arrêts du petit chemin de fer" (2: 1110). The trajectory of the train suggests novelty, the changes in life, the passing of time and space. It is both a positive suggestion, representing travel (both in the world and in "the countryside of the self") and a negative one, suggesting the transience of the world, the jealous sado-masochistic relationships, the dissimulation and uncertainty inherent in society. However, it is the novelty of the experience of riding in an automobile that captures Proust's imagination. It is in the novelty, the freedom of this newly emerging means of transportation that Proust truly expresses his world view. The change from train to automobile gives Proust an added freedom both in time (with a taxi and driver at his disposition) and space (no longer limited to the linear trajectory of a train, with its fixed itinerary).

3. Automobiles

Proust's use and enjoyment of automobiles is well known. Throughout his later life his automobile and driver served as nearly the only means of escape from the seclusion of his bedroom. In an automobile he could go where he wanted, when he wanted and, if necessary, remain insulated from whatever it was he had gone to see (for instance from flowers, to which he was allergic). The automobile was his own little enclosed world. As Léon Pierre-Quint writes:

> Sa sensibilité avait de tels raffinements dans la souffrance qu'on ne le prenait pas au sérieux. Quand, saisi du désir nostalgique de revoir des aubépines, des nymphéas, il se faisait conduire à la campagne dans une voiture complètement fermée et qu'il se contentait de regarder les champs et les bois par les vitres, ses amis pensaient accompagner un malade imaginaire.[12]

According to Painter, Proust was feeling relatively good at Cabourg, in August of 1912. Even his sleeping habits had improved. His friends were there and he was adapting to the external world fairly well. Despite his friends' misfortunes behind the wheel, he was enjoying riding around the countryside in Normandy and would not let a few rather depressing incidents stop him:

> But his ardour was chilled by a series of disasters: on the 11th Nahmias ran over a poor little girl, who died two days later, on the road to Caen; on the 25th Bardac killed another outright; and a few days later two local taxis were wrecked in a collision. In the end he prudently hired the hotel omnibus—"it's enormous and far from elegant," he told Mme Straus, "but it's safe, and the driver is very careful and clever." (2: 180)

The change from the use of carriages to the ever more common use of automobiles in Proust's lifetime is reflected in a passage found at the end of *Du côté de chez Swann* at the Bois de Boulogne. The narrator is forced to face not only the reality of the passing of time, but also of place. Both time and place are thin, unconnected, juxtaposed and irretrievable slices. First he is horrified and unaccepting, then defeated and suffering. The whole experience is punctuated dramatically (almost theatrically one might say) by a series of "Hélas" and "Quelle horreur":

> Quelle horreur! me disais-je: peut-on trouver ces automobiles élégantes comme étaient les anciens attelages? je suis sans doute déjà trop vieux.... Les lieux que nous avons connus n'appartiennent pas qu'au monde de l'espace où nous les situons pour plus de facilité. Ils n'étaient qu'une mince tranche au milieu d'impressions contiguës qui formaient notre vie d'alors; le souvenir d'une certaine image n'est que le regret d'un certain instant; et les maisons, les routes, les avenues, sont fugitives, hélas! comme les années. (1: 427)

For Marcel, however, the automobile has another significance. Having one becomes an essential factor in his relationship with Albertine. Now they are able to visit more places in one day than they could have before in two. Time and space have changed for them: "La figure du pays nous semblait toute changée tant, dans l'image topographique que nous faisons de chacun d'eux, la notion d'espace est loin d'être celle qui joue le plus grand rôle. Nous avons dit que celle du temps les écarte davantage" (2: 1004).

As we have seen with the other technological developments, the effect is a double one; it first helps to explore the farthest reaches of the world (as we see here) and then reveals the uncertainty, the instability, the relativity involved in such an exploration of the physical universe. The experience of riding in an automobile also does to the mystery of place what Brichot did to the mystery of name during the conversation in the train:

> Mais l'automobile ... ne respecte aucun mystère.... Il peut sembler que mon amour pour les féeriques voyages en chemin de fer aurait dû m'empêcher de partager l'émerveillement d'Albertine devant l'automobile qui mène, même un malade, là où il veut, et empêche—comme je l'avais fait jusqu'ici—de considérer l'emplacement comme la marque individuelle, l'essence sans succédané des beautés inamovibles. (2: 1005)

The particular individuality of place—for Marcel its beauty—is no longer part of its essence. The particular, sesame-like entrance into a place through the portals of the train station, and the idyllic continuation of the mystery of place is no longer part of the travel experience:

> Et sans doute, cet emplacement, l'automobile n'en faisait pas, comme jadis le chemin de fer, quand j'étais venu de Paris à Balbec, un but soustrait aux contingences de la vie ordinaire, presque idéal au départ et qui, le restant à l'arrivée, à l'arrivée dans cette grande demeure où n'habite personne et qui porte seulement le nom de la ville, la gare, a l'air d'en promettre enfin l'accessibilité, comme elle en serait la matérialisation. (2: 1005)

The automobile circles, spirals in like an animal closing in on its prey. It is a more precise instrument of exploration than the train. Another mystery is lost and more knowledge gained. It does not lead them "féeriquement" into a city, but does offer new perspectives in its narrowing circles. The world is still in movement, the city "fuyait dans tous les sens pour échapper." But to no avail, for the automobile finally reaches its target. The experience with the automobile gives the impression of having helped the traveller feel, "d'une main plus amoureusement exploratrice, avec une plus fine précision, la véritable géométrie, la belle 'mesure de la terre' " (2: 1006). The importance of this change from an essentially linear to a circular vision will be discussed shortly.

In comparing the automobile to the train, we see Proust adding another level to his series of effects, that is, from the mystery of a voyage in a train, to its loss in the precision of the movements of the auto, to a new sense of instability, relativity, followed by a new mystery, a new sense of certainty in the creative rush he has. As Pichois notes, the consequences—geographic, sociological, and aesthetic—of this new world view result in a new psychology: "Le dépaysement, l'effet d'étrangeté dû à la vitesse permettent de modifier les conditions de la perception, les catégories du temps et de l'espace, de briser cet 'agrégat de raisonnements' dont est faite notre perception, de désintellectualiser celle-ci, en un mot de retrouver la fraîcheur de la sensation. Vitesse, dans ce cas c'est poésie" (93).

The word—the foundation of art as expressed through language—is the tool, then, that will break Marcel out of his confinement in time, space, and self, and in which he will find a new certainty, a new order, a new world view. The sense of mystery and of freedom in a name, a word, that Brichot destroyed in his etymological discussions is reborn here, in this artistic flight. From the loss of the mystery in a name on the train, to an exploration in the place with the automobile, with a similar loss in mystery and meaning, to an unexpected experience in the place that will engender a new mystery, a new meaning, expressed in the word—which can be anything from little Marcel's "zut!," (1: 155) to the piece given in the description of the steeples, to the entire work itself. Though meaning is not to be found in the place, the thing itself, it is only through a novel experience with the place, the thing that this new certainty can be born. It is not surprising, then, that the place, the thing (here, the steeples), seem to "contain" and "hide" this new meaning: "En constatant, en notant la forme de leur flèche, le déplacement de leurs lignes, l'ensoleillement de leur surface, je sentais que je n'allais pas au bout de mon impression, que quelque chose était derrière ce mouvement, derrière cette clarté, quelque chose qu'ils semblaient contenir et dérober à la fois" (1: 180).

The narrator has wanted to be a writer for a long time, waiting until he finds a subject of infinite philosophical meaning before he begins. This conscious effort of intellect and will leads the narrator nowhere, making him think, in fact, that he must have a physical or mental deficiency. Proust's black humor is evident as the narrator concludes that, since he wants to be a writer, it is time that he decides what he is going to write about: "Mais dès que je me le demandais, tâchant de trouver un sujet où je pusse faire tenir une signification philosophique infinie, mon esprit s'arrêtait de fonctionner, je ne voyais plus que le vide en face de mon attention, je sentais que je n'avais pas de génie ou peut-être une maladie cérébrale l'empêchait de naître" (1: 173) He had hoped there would be some help from above; from one of the accepted authorities of God, country, and family and asks self-mockingly: "... peut-être cette absence de génie, ce trou noir qui se creusait dans mon esprit quand je cherchais le sujet de mes écrits futurs, n'était-il aussi qu'une illusion sans consistance, et cesserait-elle par l'intervention de mon père qui avait dû convenir avec le Gouvernement et avec la Providence que je serais le premier écrivain de l'époque" (1: 173). With the expected failure of these ironic appeals to an external authority, he renounces literature forever and accepts his own earthbound, limited existence; a boring life with no meaning, no magic. It seems to him that he is like any other person who will get old and die: "Ce sentiment intime, immédiat, que j'avais du néant de ma pensée, prévalait contre toutes les paroles flatteuses qu'on pouvait me prodiguer comme, chez un méchant dont chacun vante les bonnes actions, les remords de sa conscience" (1: 173-74). Marcel's search for certainty has apparently failed. Life has no meaning, no order, no certainty.

Then, unexpectedly, Marcel encounters a particular object—here, the steeples—an object lacking in any abstract significance for him. In this experience Marcel finds meaning, pleasure and power:

> Certes ce n'était pas des impressions de ce genre qui pouvaient me rendre l'espérance que j'avais perdue de pouvoir être un jour écrivain et poète, car elles étaient toujours liées à un objet particulier dépourvu de valeur intellectuelle et ne se rapportant à aucune vérité abstraite. Mais du moins elles me donnaient un plaisir irraisonné, l'illusion d'une sorte de fécondité et par là me distrayaient de l'ennui, du sentiment de mon impuissance que j'avais éprouvés chaque fois que j'avais cherché un sujet philosophique pour une grande œuvre littéraire. (1: 179)

As we shall see, though rejecting the external authority and certainty found in a God on high, it is through his symbolic, material manifestation on earth, the steeples of Martinville, (or "le doigt levé de dieu," as the narrator calls the steeple of Saint-Hilaire [1: 66]) that Marcel will experience a new certainty, a new order, a new unity, coming from the depths of the self. The "secours d'en haut" is actually a "secours d'en bas." There is Grace, but there is no God.

4. Airplanes

Though it seems out of character for Marcel (not to mention Proust), he goes on a horse-back ride through a "wild route" to see the Verdurins at Rivebelle. Marcel is in another universe, recognizing the countryside as that in one of Elstir's paintings: "Leur souvenir replaçait les lieux où je me trouvais tellement en dehors du monde actuel que je n'aurais pas été étonné si, comme le jeune homme de l'âge antéhistorique que peint Elstir, j'avais, au cours de ma promenade, croisé un personnage mythologique" (2: 1029). Marcel encounters more novelty and surprise than he expected in this already unaccustomed act when he hears what will be his first airplane. All of a sudden, his horse bolts at hearing a strange sound. Marcel tries to control him, and not be thrown to the ground. He looks up, his eyes full of tears and sees, about fifty meters above him, "dans le soleil, entre deux grandes ailes d'acier étincelant qui l'emportaient, un être dont la figure peu distincte me parut ressembler à celle d'un homme" (2: 1029). He encounters his "personnage mythologique" in the pilot of the airplane, and is moved to tears as he feels the sense of novelty, freedom and liberation (while he, on the other hand, is earthbound, imprisoned by habit): "Je fus aussi ému que pouvait l'être un Grec qui voyait pour la première fois un demi-dieu. Je pleurais aussi, car j'étais prêt à pleurer du moment que j'avais reconnu que le bruit venait d'au-dessus de ma tête ... à la pensée que ce que j'allais voir pour la première fois c'était un aéroplane" (2: 1029). This "demi-god" seems to break even the law of gravity, following a sort of inverted law of gravity:

> Cependant l'aviateur sembla hésiter sur sa voie; je sentais ouvertes devant lui—devant moi, si l'habitude ne m'avait pas fait prisonnier— toutes les routes de l'espace, de la vie; il poussa plus loin, plana quelques instants au-dessus de la mer, puis prenant brusquement son parti, semblant céder à quelque attraction inverse de celle de la pesanteur, comme retournant dans sa patrie, d'un léger mouvement de ses ailes d'or il piqua droit vers le ciel. (2: 1029)

According to Proust's young friend, Marcel Plantevignes, it was his own equestrian experience at Cabourg which inspired the writer[13]:

> Le soir, encore tout ému et tout chaud de cette péripétie, ce fût la première chose que je contais à Proust, lui marquant l'angoisse que j'avais ressentie de me sentir aussi désarmé devant cette peur nouvelle d'apocalypse qui semblait tombée du ciel pour mon cheval affolé.
> Et Proust, frappé en effet par la nouveauté de cette impression de peur tombant du ciel me demanda la permission de s'en approprier la description comme étant arrivée à lui et d'y faire allusion dans ses écrits, —ce à quoi naturellement je consentis. Et en effet dans *Sodome et Gomorrhe,* Proust parle de cet incident équestre à la première personne comme arrivé à lui. (352)

The incident described here provided not only the background for the passage mentioned above, but can also be seen as a seed of the highly apocalyptic passage surrounding the incident in Jupien's sadist house, where confusion has hit an entire city and the plane has become a squadron bringing death. Here again, Proust shows he is aware of the importance of a change which will affect not only man's life, but also his world view. Confined, earthbound, limited, the beauty and exhilaration of the feeling of flight had an undeniable appeal to Proust, and is reflected in *A la recherche du temps perdu.* As Plantevignes notes, Proust was already interested in this important development before his description of his equestrian experience:

> D'ailleurs, d'une façon générale, Proust suivait avec émoi les progrès de l'aviation naissante, et un soir,—aux alentours de 1910,—dans sa chambre du Grand Hôtel de Cabourg, comme nous devisions tranquillement, un avion important tout bruissant d'un bruit apocalyptique, et semblant avoir rasé de près l'hôtel, tant il volait bas, passa avec fracas au-dessus de nous dans le ciel nocturne, nous coupant la parole, et Proust, alerté, s'interrompant soudain de ce à quoi il songeait, et me désignant d'un doigt dramatique le bruit et le ciel, me dit gravement:
> —Ecoutez Marcel, écoutez, les temps futurs qui sont en marche! (352-53)

The introduction of airplanes into the world of *A la recherche du temps perdu* on a large scale occurs in the last volume, *Le Temps retrouvé*. It is World War I and the darkness of the night is augmented by the blackout of the city lights. The advent of war has precipitated the use of the airplane. Proust is conscious of both the beauty and the death it represents. He is conscious also of its intrusion into the one area of apparent stability and unchanging order to which man has looked since the times of the Babylonians: the stars. Speaking to Robert de Saint-Loup, Marcel describes the beauty in the ascent of the planes, when they become part of the constellations, obeying man's laws, as precise as those of the immutable stars: "Je reconnais que c'est très beau le moment où ils montent, où [les avions] vont *faire constellation,* et obéissent en cela à des lois tout aussi précises que celles qui régissent les constellations, car ce qui te semble un spectacle est le ralliement des escadrilles, les commandements qu'on leur donne, leur départ en chasse, etc." (3: 758). Marcel's interest in the beauty of the airplanes' ascent and inclusion in the celestial clockwork is only surmounted by their breaking of these laws, by their moving and, hence, the destruction of the immutable, unchanging order of the cosmos. The Greek god described earlier in the novel is now seen more in the Germanic tradition:

> Mais est-ce que tu n'aimes pas mieux le moment où, définitivement assimilés aux étoiles, ils s'en détachent pour partir en chasse ou rentrer après la berloque, le moment où ils *font apocalypse,* même les étoiles ne gardant plus leur place? Et ces sirènes, était-ce assez wagnérien, ce qui, du reste, était bien naturel pour saluer l'arrivée des Allemands, ça faisait très hymne national, avec le Kronprinz et les princesses dans la loge impériale, *Wacht am Rhein;* c'était à se demander si c'était bien des aviateurs et pas plutôt des Walkyries qui montaient." (3: 758)

It is no longer only the immediate physical world that is in movement; now the stars, the sky are also. The personification has reached outward to the limits of the visible universe. The stars are like insects or "human shooting stars." Instead of drawing order, meaning and certainty down from the heavens, man's ordering reason is projected upward and outward:

> La plus grande impression de beauté que nous faisaient éprouver ces étoiles humaines et filantes, était peut-être surtout de faire regarder le ciel, vers lequel on lève peu les yeux d'habitude. Dans ce Paris dont, en 1914, j'avais vu la beauté presque sans défense attendre la menace de l'ennemi qui se rapprochait, il y avait certes, maintenant comme alors, la splendeur antique inchangée d'une lune cruellement, mystérieusement sereine [mais] il y avait aussi autre chose, des lumières différentes, des feux intermittents que, soit de ces aéroplanes, soit de projecteurs de la Tour Eiffel, on savait dirigés par une volonté intelligente. . . . (3: 801)

The familiarity of an old and unchanging sky is replaced by beauty in the novelty of the planes. The feeling of security that was previously found in a stable, unchanging universe is replaced by confidence in man's intelligence, his will, and their manifestations on the macrocosmic level in the form of the government and the military. These willfull, intellectual intrusions into the sky, while bringing a certain sense of security, are still unsettling, making the narrator feel he is not even in the same world. It is as if the earth has moved under his feet, as if he were in a different part of the world, under "new stars." The sky is in more motion than the earth.

> Des aéroplanes montaient encore comme des fusées rejoindre les étoiles, et des projecteurs promenaient lentement, dans le ciel sectionné, comme une pâle poussière d'astres, d'errantes voies lactées. Cependant les aéroplanes venaient s'insérer au milieu des constellations et on aurait pu se croire dans un autre hémisphère en effet, en voyant ces "étoiles nouvelles." (3: 801-02)

The mixed, paradoxical emotions are typically Proustian. The airplane represents both beauty and death. The security and familiarity of the unchanging sky are replaced by novelty and fear, while, at the same time, they represent man's finite yet noble effort (suggested by the lines of light projected into the infinite darkness). Marcel is not truly aware of the death and tragedy the planes bring until he actually sees a bomb dropped near the fountains of the Champs-Elysées and the Place de la Concorde:

> Car la réalité originale d'un danger n'est perçue que dans cette chose nouvelle, irréductible à ce qu'on sait déjà, qui s'appelle une impression, et qui est souvent, comme ce fut le cas là, résumée par une ligne, une ligne qui décrivait une intention . . . autour de l'aéroplane menaçant et traqué . . . les jets d'eau lumineux des projecteurs s'infléchissaient dans le ciel, lignes pleines d'intentions aussi, d'intentions prévoyantes et protectrices, d'hommes puissants et sages. . . . (3: 802)

The airplane, the greatest articulation of man's intelligence, of his technical ability to travel in and master the physical, mechanistic universe, breaks even the most fundamental laws of gravity. It represents man's pride, power, security, and finally, death.

It is here, in war-time Paris, that Marcel will follow "l'inverti" Charlus into Jupien's sexually inverted house. While showing the universality of the vice of inversion, with a suggestion of sarcasm directed toward the members of the church, it is not without humor that the narrator describes an encounter between Jupien and a client who may be seen as Jupien's religious counterpart:

> . . . j'aperçus entrer avec une démarche lente, à côté d'un militaire qui évidemment sortait avec elle d'une chambre voisine, une personne qui me parut une dame assez âgée, en jupe noire. Je reconnus bientôt mon erreur, c'était un prêtre . . . un mauvais prêtre. . . . et levant vers son visage hideux un doigt de docteur en théologie, dit sentencieusement: "Que voulez-vous, je ne suis pas (j'attendais 'un saint') une ange." (3: 829)

After having excused his unorthodox and—according to the teachings of the church—immoral behavior, the priest tries to break even the one law of Jupien's establishment: he tries to slip out without paying his bill:

> D'ailleurs il n'avait plus qu'à s'en aller et prit congé de Jupien qui, ayant accompagné le baron, venait de remonter, mais par étourderie le mauvais prêtre oublia de payer sa chambre. Jupien, que son esprit n'abandonnait jamais, agita le tronc dans lequel il mettait la contribution de chaque client, et le fit sonner en disant: "Pour les frais du culte, Monsieur l'abbé!" Le vilain personnage s'excusa, donna sa pièce et disparut. (3: 829)

Besides a sense of humor, with a sarcasm directed principally towards the hypocritical (and cheap) priest, Proust shows a certain sympathy for his families' former gardener, this male "madame." Marcel refers to Jupien's establishment as a theater of madmen. Like Charlus, he gives himself the noble (and merely observational) role of calif. In a sense, he has reversed the movement from legend to sexual hell, reinfusing the scene with references to the Oriental and mysterious *Mille et une Nuits*. He reinforces both the legendary and the demonic aspects of this scene with a subtle reference to Western tradition in proclaiming Jupien's establishment "a true pandemonium." The origin of the suffix of this word is the Greek word "daimon," meaning demon, spirit, or deity. Milton used the word "pandaemonium" as the name of the capital of hell in *Paradise Lost*. East meets West.

> "En attendant, dis-je à Jupien, cette maison est tout autre chose, plus qu'une maison de fous, puisque la folie des aliénés qui y habitent est mise en scène, reconstituée, visible, c'est un vrai pandemonium. J'avais cru comme le calife des *Mille et une Nuits* arriver à point au secours d'un homme qu'on frappait, et c'est un autre conte des *Mille et une Nuits* que j'ai vu réalisé devant moi, celui où une femme, transformée en chienne, se fait frapper volontairement pour retrouver sa forme première." (3: 832)

Jupien speaks Marcel's language when he responds to the latter's reference to *Mille et une Nuits* with one of his own. The interplay between imagination and reality (from the images of the magic lantern to the "sexual hell" seen through the peephole to the allusions to *Mille et une Nuits*) is further compounded by Jupien's reference to a translation of Ruskin's *Sésame et les Lys* that Marcel had sent to Charlus. Jupien's little enclosed world (as he points out in his play on words) is his magical domain, open only on his command, as in the story of "Ali-Baba and the Forty Thieves." Jupien and Marcel also seem to share an interest in windows, and their importance in their respective "little enclosed worlds":

> "Vous parlez de bien des contes des *Mille et une Nuits,* me dit-il. Mais j'en connais un qui n'est pas sans rapport avec le titre d'un livre que je crois avoir aperçu chez le baron (il faisait allusion à une traduction de *Sésame et les Lys* de Ruskin que j'avais envoyée à M. de Charlus). Si jamais vous étiez curieux, un soir, de voir, je ne dis pas quarante, mais une dizaine de voleurs, vous n'avez qu'à venir ici; pour savoir si je suis

> là vous n'avez qu'à regarder la fenêtre de là-haut, je laisse ma petite fenêtre ouverte et éclairée, cela veut dire que je suis venu, qu'on peut entrer; c'est mon Sésame à moi. Je dis seulement Sésame. Car pour les Lys, si c'est eux que vous voulez, je vous conseille d'aller les chercher ailleurs." (3: 832-33)

As Marcel and Jupien start to take leave after this witty and imaginative conversation, their little world of Persian princes and pirates is bombarded by the airplanes. Death is everywhere: from the heavens outside in the general attack of the airplanes—to the most particular and personal manifestation in the form of a little cross Marcel finds on the floor (left there by Robert de Saint-Loup not long before his death at the front).

From this little enclosed world where the deepest of sexual desires may be realized, Marcel travels into even deeper, darker recesses of the self, when he enters the pitch-black subway to escape the airplanes. Marcel loses his way in the darkened, bombarded streets. He thinks back to the first day he saw the airplane, when it was a sort of Greek god. The inverted symbolism of the airplane becomes apparent to him as he realizes now that it has become the god of evil bringing death:

> En un instant, les rues devinrent entièrement noires. Parfois seulement, un avion ennemi qui volait assez bas éclairait le point où il voulait jeter une bombe. Je ne retrouvais plus mon chemin. Je pensai à ce jour, en allant à la Raspelière, où j'avais rencontré, comme un dieu qui avait fait se cabrer mon cheval, un avion. Je pensais que maintenant la rencontre serait différente et que le dieu du mal me tuerait. (3: 833)

Marcel hurries to escape, turning "en cercles dans les places noires," recalling either Dante's hell, or Daedelus's labyrinth. He thinks of Jupien's house, perhaps destroyed by now, and contemplates the apocalyptic last moments of Pompei: ". . . cette maison sur laquelle M. de Charlus eût pu prophétiquement écrire 'Sodoma' comme avait fait, avec non moins de prescience ou peut-être au début de l'éruption volcanique et de la catastrophe déjà commencée, l'habitant inconnu de Pompéi" (3: 833).

Later, riding in the streets of Paris, faced with the destruction of the world he used to know and all the novelty, all the change, the unfamiliar surroundings that had earlier brought on so much anguish, Marcel experiences another of those sudden, magical feelings that transform the world. Change, motion, novelty: all the things that previously brought on uncertainty and fear are now accepted. He can now adapt to the unfamiliarity of the external world. His separation and confinement from the external world, itself divided into little enclosed worlds, little slices in time and space divided by what Poulet refers to as "the principle of discontinuity," is transcended. He uses the experience of riding in an automobile to explain the sensation. It is the experience of a fundamental change in the world he is moving in. The ground on which his automobile is rolling changes from paving stones (divided, as are time and space in the world view just described) into a finer, smoother ride on sand, or dead leaves. Time and space are no longer divided into little parcels. The self is no longer contained and isolated. It is one continuous ride, the "principle of discontinuity" has been transcended and the chains of the contingencies of a world fixed in a mechanistic universe are broken. In another inverted image, Proust moves from the automobile to the airplane and uses the latter not to suggest death, but rather the resurrecting flight of memory. Riding down streets he used to take with Françoise on his way to the Champs-Elysées, but had forgotten: "Le sol de lui-même savait où aller; sa résistance était vaincu. Et, comme un aviateur qui a jusque-là péniblement roulé à terre, "décollant" brusquement, je m'élevais lentement vers les hauteurs silencieuses du souvenir" (3: 858).

Contrary to what one might think, then, hearing from the sedentary narrator of the first pages of *Du côté de chez Swann,* motion is a fundamental aspect of Proust's work. He must travel. Sleep, drugs, memory and, in particular, "le plaisir spécial" send him inward, into "le paysage du moi," each with a change in speed of the mechanism of the body. Due to technological developments of the times, he is allowed to go farther, faster, and higher than was previously possible in man's history. In the internal world of the self, the traveller, Marcel—having escaped both the confines of his room and those of the finite, positivistic world, based on causality and fixed references in time and space—must find a new way of looking at things, a new methodology, a new set of tools and standards in his search for certainty in this world where subject and object are one.

Moving outward, away from his room, Marcel encounters novelty in a series of sensorial contacts with the particulars of reality—the smell of the varnish of the stairway leading from Marcel's room to downstairs, the taste of the madeleine and herbal tea in the living room, the sight of the light on the lines of the steeples of Martinville and Vieuxvicq—all of which provide him with the excitement necessary for the memories which will make up his "édifice immense du souvenir." In the movement outward one sees another aspect in this search for certainty, that is, with these sensorial contacts, Marcel is able to be sure that what he experiences is the real, external world and not simply a projection of his own imagination, like that of the magic lantern onto Marcel's bedroom wall. He must prove that it has body, that it is not simply a play of light, but also has a physical, objective reality.

As technology develops, so does man's relationship to the world. Time and space take on new meaning as one moves from carriage to train to automobile to airplane. As Marcel reaches the speed of the train and automobile in his search for certainty in the external world of objects, he finds them as unfamiliar and in motion as in the first pages of *A la recherche du temps perdu*. The search has not helped to find certainty, but ends up in the whirlpool of the Einsteinian world view of relativity. In the outward search for certainty, for life, science and technology once again lead to uncertainty and, as seen in the apocalyptic passage with the airplanes, to death. Paradoxically, at each experience of speed, of novelty, another brick is made for his "édifice immense du souvenir," the foundation for the narrator's new certainty. Marcel begins to write when he observes the steeples of Martinville and Vieuxvicq while riding with Dr. Percepied. His experiences in the world arouse the "plaisir spécial," transporting him into the world of the self, outside the contingencies of time and space, where he finds the essence of a new world view, a new certainty. The previously apocalyptic airplane finally represents the magical, resurrecting flight of memory and, in the final analysis, the artist himself.[14]

✦   ✦   ✦

IV

Proust and the Human Sciences

IN *A LA RECHERCHE DU TEMPS PERDU,* the narrator's search for certainty in the external world leads him repeatedly back to the individual. The narrator's efforts to understand the laws of the immediate physical world and, reaching even farther out, of the celestial mechanics, lead only to further uncertainty. The order he hopes to find in the objective, empirical world is inextricably bound to the subject doing the searching. To find meaning in man's world one must understand both the world and man.

The narrator looks at man both as species and as individual. He considers him both as a physical being, manifesting laws in the objective world, and as a metaphysical or spiritual being, manifesting laws in the subjective world. In so doing, the scientist, looking for empirical laws in an objective universe, using his intellect and reason, must join with the artist who, using intuition, follows a different methodology in his own search in man's internal landscape. A "grave uncertainty" experienced by the narrator while experimenting with the madeleine and herbal tea grows from his realization of the need for a new methodology: "Je pose la tasse et me tourne vers mon esprit. C'est à lui de trouver la vérité. Mais comment? Grave incertitude, toutes les fois que l'esprit se sent dépassé par lui-même; quand lui, le chercheur, est tout ensemble le pays obscur où il doit chercher et où tout son bagage ne lui sera de rien. Chercher? pas seulement: créer" (1: 45). Thus, while the narrator considers man as a naturalist (that is, as a physical being obeying objective, verifiable laws) he will finally turn his vision to man's internal, subjective world, the domain of the psychologist and artist (two not so dissimilar professions, as we shall see). It is in this inversion of the search that André Maurois sees the essential theme of *A la recherche du temps perdu:*

> Le sujet central de son roman ne sera ni la peinture d'une certaine société française à la fin du dix-neuvième siècle, ni une nouvelle analyse de l'amour . . . mais la lutte de l'Esprit contre le Temps, l'impossibilité de trouver dans la vie réelle un point fixe auquel le moi se puisse accrocher, le devoir de trouver ce point fixe en soi-même, la possibilité de le trouver dans l'œuvre d'art. Voilà le thème essentiel, profond et neuf, de la *Recherche du Temps Perdu*.[1]

Proust's interest in and knowledge of the human sciences—medicine, biology, sociology and psychology—are well established. We shall consider these influences and their manifestations in his book, *A la recherche du temps perdu*. In discussing the latter we shall follow the movement already suggested, that is, from outward to inward, from telescopic to microscopic, from general to particular. One's vision is turned inward, from the stars, to the physical boundaries of man's immediate experience in the physical world, to man in his objective or physical being. What are the laws governing man's body? We shall then look further inward, into the "landscape of the self," moving (as if one were following the shape of an hourglass) from the particular to the general, from the individual and subjective, to the universal and objective (or whatever its equivalent would be in this internal universe of the self). In this way we shall see if the narrator succeeds in his search for certainty. If so, on what is this certainty founded? How does it manifest itself in his book, and according to what laws does it operate?

1. The Background

The causes of Proust's interest in science are varied, and have been traced to both individual influences (e.g., teachers, authors, family, friends) and to a general "spirit of the times." The influence of his philosophy teacher, Alphonse Darlu (said to be an inspiration for the writer Bergotte in Proust's novel), can be seen in "the very core of the novel." Darlu taught him a paradoxical view of the world, showing him "the importance of scientific discovery, ('How agreeable it would be, to be a really intelligent scientist and get to the bottom of these things' Darlu would say) or the 'unreality of the sensible world.' "[2]

One of the more famous of Proust's possible influences was Henri Bergson. That Marcel Proust was aware of his work there can be no doubt. Aside from being related to Bergson by marriage, some critics argue that

Proust had read Bergson's writings and had even studied under him at the Sorbonne (although Bergson never held a post there). Roger Shattuck argues that Proust must have read *Matière et mémoire:* "[Bergson's] *Matter and Memory* appeared with great éclat when Proust was twenty-five. Its blend of phenomenological description, scientific attitude, philosophical intent, and lucid style must have been irresistible to a young author who was already absorbed in closely related problems of subjective experience."[3] Joyce Megay, however, argues convincingly against such an enthusiasm on Proust's part: "Visiblement, Bergson n'était pas au centre des préoccupations de Proust au moment où celui-ci se mettait à composer *La Recherche*."[4] Megay also maintains that Proust had a limited knowledge of Bergson's writings (17). As early as November 12, 1913, in an interview with the newspaper *Le Temps,* Proust himself—while acknowledging a common interest—makes a distinction between his novel and the work of Bergson: "Mon livre serait peut-être comme un essai d'une suite de *romans de l'inconscient;* je n'aurais aucune honte à dire de *romans bergsoniens* si je le croyais, mais ce ne serait pas exact" (Maurois 287). While this in itself does not preclude parallels (many of which have been made), another, less discussed source for Proust's interests has recently been shown to be of perhaps greater value. In her work *Marcel Proust: théories pour une esthétique,* Anne Henry makes a convincing case for a Germanic influence on Proust. Though Henry mentions several German philosophers (including Schelling, Schlegel, and Kant) Schopenhauer is the most discussed. With his "kantisme chaleureux," Darlu was probably the source of this not so general knowledge.[5] While studying theories of perception, dreams, memory, the self, the reality of the external world and of space and time with his philosophy professor, Proust began the development of his theories (Maurois 212). As George Poulet points out, "Si le temps proustien prend toujours la forme de l'espace, c'est qu'il est d'une nature telle qu'il est directement opposé au temps bergsonien."[6] For Proust, Henry argues, the opposition is not a mechanistic one between body and soul, as it appears in Bergson's works. It is, rather, a Schopenhauerian one between Nature and soul (340). Many terms often attributed to Bergson—including Proust's famous distinction between voluntary and involuntary memory—are derived from Schopenhauer:

> Toutefois ni la conception de la mémoire ni celle du fond premier de perceptions . . . ni la disqualification de l'intelligence pratique et des catégories de la représentation n'appartiennent en propre à Bergson—pas plus que "durée" et "étendue" ou "données immédiates de la conscience."

> Proust puise directement dans Schopenhauer et son appropriation lui
> apparaît avec raison totalement personnelle. (Henry 333)

If the influence is so strong, so direct, why does Proust not acknowledge it? He only mentions Schopenhauer twice in his novel (both times as a sign of Mme de Cambremer's remarkable intelligence) (3: 739, 993). Though there are only three references to Schopenhauer in Proust's (published) correspondence, they suggest a familiarity with Schopenhauer's philosophy. In 1905 he writes to Mme de Noailles of Schopenhauer's theory concerning the unity of the world.[7] In 1906 he flatters Robert de Montesquiou with the expressed regret that his friend's letter, while more profound than Schopenhauer's theory, should be reserved for only himself alone (*Correspondance VI* 353). In 1911 he makes a reference to Schopenhauer's *Métaphysique de la Musique* in a letter to the musician Reynaldo Hahn, a friend with whom he often discussed music theory (*Correspondance X* 332). Nowhere, however, is there a clear acknowledgement of his debt to either the Germans in general, or Schopenhauer in particular. And why have so few critics discussed the German roots of Proust's theories?

The answers to both questions appear to be similar, and perhaps have to do with the French prejudices against the Germans. The narrator speaks of Robert de Saint-Loup's unusual intelligence and independence of spirit, manifested in his many Germanic references, in the same way as he referred to Mme de Cambremer. One simply did not speak of the Germans. While aware of contemporary German thought, the typical French pedant showed little sympathy for German influences: "D'ailleurs [Brichot] avait peu de sympathie pour la Nouvelle Sorbonne où les idées d'exactitude scientifique, à l'allemande, commençaient à l'emporter sur l'humanisme" (2: 868). Even such a major reference work as Micheline Tison-Braun's *La crise de l'humanisme* does not mention Schopenhauer or Schelling.[8] Add to this reluctance to speak of the Germans the presumed difficulty of the language and the comfortable comparisons with Bergson, and one can better understand perhaps why this particular past has not been as fully researched as it might have been.

The background of Proust's interest in medicine is particularly easy to trace. The influence of his father and brother cannot be ignored. Both were doctors. His father was one of the leading men of medicine in France and in 1866 established a *cordon sanitaire* against cholera. This resulted in a concern with both a global view of the world and an ability to communicate this view to the politicians (Painter 2: 2). According to George Painter, the Spanish tour taken by the narrator's father with M. de Norpois in *A l'ombre* (1: 701) is based on the investigation of an outbreak of cholera led by Dr. Proust (Painter 2: 78). Ironically, it was through his interest in pathology that Adrien Proust became involved in the newly emerging science of psychology. Of the different clinics developing in Paris during the 1880s one (whose directors were Pierre Janet and J. M. Charcot) was staffed with pathologists. Through Charcot's clinic, Dr. Proust became involved in the study of hypnotic sleep, and eventually took a patient's case ("Emile X") to the "Académie des sciences morales" (86). Pierre Janet, who is citing Broussais's *De l'irritation et de la folie,* states that "l'homme n'est connu qu'à moitié, s'il n'est observé que dans l'état sain; l'état de maladie fait aussi bien partie de son existence morale que de son existence physique."[9] To the artist this offers a new, "scientific" methodology for his search in the human landscape. However, as we have seen in the optical and physical sciences, the results of this new "objective" methodology often seem more religious or occult than scientific: "Et alors, pour un moment, quelques [écrivains comme] Proust . . . conçoivent l'espoir que cette jeune science qui, tout en se basant sur l'observation la plus rigoureuse, sur l'expérimentation la plus impartiale, s'est faite le bastion de l'antirationalisme, deviendra le fondement d'une métaphysique, ou—qui sait?—d'une religion nouvelle."[10] While the artists looked to the psychologists for a scientific methodology, the psychologists looked to the artists as rare subjects of observation in their own search for the laws governing the internal countryside of man.

Proust's personal knowledge of the work being done by Charcot and the others was not limited to that gained through his father. He was also very close to the Daudet family, who themselves had ties with their neighbor, Charcot (Czoniczer 35). Léon Daudet, who was studying to be a doctor at the time, was personally interested in this new shared ground between scientist and artist, as one sees in this observation:

> Touchant ainsi au plus secret des êtres, la médecine a de nombreux points de contact avec la littérature, et Charcot n'avait pas en principe une mauvaise idée, lorsqu'il cherchait à les associer dans une société de psycho-physiologie. . . . C'est à ma connaissance, une des rares tentatives de collaboration qui aient été faites, entre l'observation clinique et l'observation tout court.[11]

Thanks to Charcot, the study of psychology was growing in popularity (Czoniczer 83). The symbiotic relationship between psychologist and artist formed the foundation for a vision of the world inside man as radically new as were the innovations in the technical and physical sciences for man's vision of the world outside. Both also provided new tools to aid in the search for laws, and both end, paradoxically, in revolutionary world views. This may help explain why, while one critic (Thibaudet) may point to Proust's "new intellectual mysticism," others "make of Proust an observer, a dispassionate observer, whether it be of himself or others, and class his findings as scientific data."[12] This is the inescapable paradox of any effort to objectively, to scientifically observe, the nature of man. How does one arrive at a rational explanation of the laws governing man's subjective nature, which is both objectively verifiable and predictable according to physical, causal, connecting principles? Is it possible to observe man's nature without distorting it—either by the subject's awareness of being observed, or by some moral interpretation on the part of the observer—invoking a psychological "principle of uncertainty"?[13] For Proust, the "whole question" lies in this problem:

> Ce qu'il y a de terrible pour l'observateur, disait-il à la fois avec l'ironie la plus déclarée et l'inquiétude d'un naturaliste savant qui craint pour la vérité et la sincérité de ses sources, c'est que toutes les vérités les plus secrètes, et donc les plus essentielles parce que les plus révélatrices,—on ne peut les apprendre que par des gens très renseignés et très peu dignes de foi. . . . Toute la question est là.[14]

Because of their relatively unguarded state, Proust even turns to drunks to arrive at the truth: "Vous savez . . . que les ivrognes sont fort intéressants à écouter, parce que c'est leur subconscient qui parle . . ." (Plantevignes 93).

Though Jacques Rivière's comparison of Proust and Freud has often been debated, there were other, "frequent mentions [and important studies] of the importance of Proust as a psychologist" (Alden 61). Aside from the particular influences of family, teacher, and friend cited above, it should also be evident that Proust's psychological inquiries were not an aberration but, rather, a reflection of the spirit of the times. The possible Freudian influences seen by some critics in *A la recherche* are due not to a direct knowledge by Proust of the psychologist's work (Freud wrote only in German, which Proust could not read) (Czoniczer 33). It is due to their shared intellectual development. As Czoniczer writes: "Si donc les lecteurs faisant connaissance en même temps avec Proust et avec Freud, leur découvraient des ressemblances, c'est que tous deux avaient développé des idées provenant de la même époque, du même milieu intellectuel . . . [c'est-à-dire] de la pensée française fin de siècle" (57).

The influences of the medical sciences on Proust's work are numerous and can be traced both to particular sources and to a general spirit of the time. It remains to be seen how these sciences manifest themselves in *A la recherche* and what role they play in his search for certainty.

2. The Pathologist

Adrien Proust's primary field of expertise manifests itself in his son's novel in a number of ways. First, Marcel Proust uses precise pathological descriptions to suggest the inescapable passing of time and as a reflection of the unobservable, internal state of an individual. In *Le Temps retrouvé*, the narrator attempts to see the order, the law working behind the destruction he sees in the faces around him. He tries to see the "curve," the "parabola" that carries people to their graves. As if he were studying a painting by Cézanne, he notes that a simple change in hair color completely alters a face that is nevertheless the same in structure. Another face impresses the narrator by its striking immobility, to such a point that it suggests an internal malady:

> [Le jeune comte] avait toujours ses traits aussi parfaitement réguliers, plus même, la rigidité physiologique de l'artério-sclérose exagérant encore la rectitude impassible de la physionomie du dandy et donnant à ces traits l'intense netteté, presque grimaçante à force d'immobilité, qu'ils auraient eue dans une étude de Mantegna ou de Michel-Ange. (3: 938)

The rectangle of his blond beard is replaced by the rectangle of a new, white beard. In the cheeks of the face of an old field marshal, the narrator sees the "savantes manipulations du temps." The geometric description continues:

> ... il lui avait fallu accomplir plus de dévastations et de reconstructions que pour mettre un dôme à la place d'une flèche, et quand on pensait qu'un pareil travail s'était opéré non sur de la matière inerte mais sur une chair qui ne change qu'insensiblement, le contraste bouleversant entre l'apparition présente et l'être que je me rappelais reculait celui-ci dans un passé plus que lointain, presque invraisemblable. (3: 941)

Proust also uses his knowledge of pathology to describe the experience of love. Again we see this major means of escape from the confines of the self cut off from the narrator (among others). Love is not a means of liberation, a source of new meaning, new certainty. Love is a disease (or, rather, a number of them). Though it is in the last few hundred pages of *A la recherche du temps perdu* that one finds the most references to medicine, specific references to love as a disease are to be found throughout the novel. Swann is in love with Odette "comme un morphinomane ou un tuberculeux" (1: 307). He is not only sick, he is addicted to the point that there is little hope for recovery: "Et de fait, l'amour de Swann en était arrivé à ce degré où le médecin et, dans certaines affections, le chirurgien le plus audacieux, se demandent si priver un malade de son vice ou lui ôter son mal, est encore raisonnable ou même possible" (1: 308). As Swann himself says: "C'est charmant, je deviens névropathe" (1: 317). Swann hopes he will live long enough for his jealousy to subside so he may be indifferent enough to ask Odette about an affair she may have had. But this, too, can only be another stage in the progression of his disease. One can never know the truth through another, above all from someone loved. Writing of the narrator's love for Gilberte, Proust describes the obstacles to truth as being like a tumor: "[Ces obstacles] ressemblent à ces tumeurs que le médecin finit par réduire mais sans en avoir connu l'origine. Comme elles ces obstacles restent mystérieux mais sont temporaires. Seulement ils durent généralement plus que l'amour" (1: 501). The narrator describes the inability of anyone to understand someone else's love as being similar to the astonishment people have in the face of a scientific fact, the cause of which remains unobservable:

> "Je trouve ridicule au fond qu'un homme de son intelligence souffre pour une personne de ce genre qui n'est même pas intéressante, car on la dit idiote," ajouta-t-elle avec la sagesse des gens non amoureux, qui trouvent qu'un homme d'esprit ne devrait être malheureux que pour une personne qui en valût la peine; c'est à peu près comme s'étonner qu'on daigne souffrir du choléra par le fait d'un être aussi petit que le bacille virgule. (1: 343)

Jealousy is also described as a physical disease: "Certes le regret d'une maîtresse, la jalousie survivante sont des maladies physiques au même titre que la tuberculose ou la leucémie" (3: 644). Infidelity is as common as a cold: ". . . chacun a sa manière d'être trahi, comme il a sa manière de s'enrhumer . . ." (3: 426). It is a complicated disease, as the source and the remedy of the problem are the same: "L'être aimé est successivement le mal et le remède qui suspend et aggrave le mal" (2: 833).

The object of love is both poison and antidote (2: 1118). Finally, as is more than evident in the story of Swann's love for Odette, love is incurable: "D'ailleurs, l'amour est un mal inguérissable, comme ces diathèses où le rhumatisme ne laisse quelque répit que pour faire place à des migraines épileptiformes" (3: 85). Marcel's disease is partially excised with Albertine's death, but it is not until the passing of time has its effects that this "maladie générale appelée amour" (2: 156) can be defeated by the "loi générale de l'oubli" (3: 644). Time kills, but it also heals.

As Serge Béhar points out, pathology plays a great role in Proust's novel. Nearly all of his characters have some kind of disease: "L'approche médicale apparaît comme le fil conducteur de l'étude du personnage."[15] Proust even situates his characters vis-à-vis their disease (Béhar 44). There remains, however, one important character who is not defined by a disease: his mother. Yet, his love for his mother is defined, in essence, by the "baiser du soir," denied little Marcel at bedtime. This denial will dominate his life, becoming at least a part of the origin of his love for Albertine: "J'embrassai [le cou d'Albertine] aussi purement que si j'avais embrassé ma mère pour calmer un chagrin d'enfant que je croyais alors ne pouvoir jamais arracher de mon cœur" (2: 1124).

Throughout his life the narrator searches for the sense of certainty lost in the denial of his mother's ritual bedtime kiss. Though well separated not only in time and space, but also in very different moral and social worlds, the description of this rather Freudian scene is strikingly similar to that of Charlus in Jupien's male brothel near the end of the novel. Both places are sources of pain for Marcel and Charlus, respectively. Both are closed, shut off from the world. In the scene with Charlus the sense of imprisonment is enhanced by the necessity of keeping all the windows shut due to the war-time blackout. An airplane pilot asks for some fresh air: " 'Si on ouvrait un peu la fenêtre, il y a une fumée ici!,' dit l'aviateur; et en effet chacun avait sa pipe ou sa cigarette. 'Oui, mais alors, fermez d'abord les volets, vous savez bien que c'est défendu d'avoir de la lumière à cause des zeppelins' " (3: 812-13). It is due in part to the stuffy air that the narrator leaves room number 43 and observes Charlus chained to his bed. As for little Marcel, even on the stairs to his room, smelling the odor of the varnish on the stairs, he experiences "l'inverse [d'un] soulagement" (1: 28). Once inside his room, the prison-like atmosphere is complete: "Une fois dans ma chambre, il fallut boucher toutes les issues, fermer les volets, creuser mon propre tombeau, en défaisant mes couvertures, revêtir le suaire de ma chemise de nuit" (1: 28). Even their beds are similar. First, Marcel's:

"Mais avant de m'ensevelir dans le lit de fer qu'on avait ajouté dans la chambre parce que j'avais trop chaud l'été sous les courtines de reps du grand lit, j'eus un mouvement de révolte, je voulus essayer d'une ruse de condamné" (1: 28). The parallel further points out the similarities between the two apparently very different passages. The origins of Charlus's tendencies are not as easily distinguishable from other people's as one might think:

> En somme son désir d'être enchaîné, d'être frappé, trahissait, dans sa laideur, un rêve aussi poétique que, chez d'autres, le désir d'aller à Venise ou d'entretenir des danseuses. Et M. de Charlus tenait tellement à ce que ce rêve lui donnât l'illusion de la réalité, que Jupien dut vendre le lit de bois qui était dans la chambre 43 et le remplacer par un lit de fer qui allait mieux avec les chaînes. (3: 840)

Thus, even the most innocent of childhood scenes and the most pure of loves are homologous to the sexual hell of Jupien's house as described in *Le Temps retrouvé*. As the reassuring certainty of the ritual bedtime kiss is replaced by the anguished uncertainty of his solitary bedroom exile, so is the poetic illusion of love succeeded by the paradoxical iron unreality of a threatening, sado-masochistic hell. Swann also inhabits this hell. Through his love for Odette he makes his descent, "comme un malade . . . dans ce nouveau cercle d'enfer d'où il n'apercevait pas comment il pourrait jamais sortir" (1: 367).

These three characters—Odette, Swann, and Charlus—represent Proust's search for laws in man's moral, sociological and biological nature. As the object of Swann's secret, enslaving desire, Odette is an example of the impossibility of a certainty based on an everlasting, shared love. However, it is in the characters of Swann and Charlus that Proust continues his investigation into the nature of man. In Swann one can see the search for natural and sociological laws and in Charlus the search for natural and psychological laws. The parallels made by Proust between the psychological patterns of the homosexual and the social position of the Jews are well documented.[16] Before turning to Proust's search for naturalistic and psychological laws one might ask why he chooses members of two such seemingly unrepresentative "races" as subjects for his inquiries into the laws of man. Both are suspect, both are judged: "de même que certains juges supposent et excusent plus facilement l'assassinat chez les invertis et la trahison chez les Juifs pour des raisons tirées du péché originel et de la fatalité de la race" (2: 615). The former stands as a quintessential representative of universal sin (Painter 2: 313), the latter as that of man's inevitable submission to racial laws.

But it is Charlus who appears at first glance to suggest the most distorted view of man. Roger Shattuck, for example, far from seeing in him the perfect specimen for Proust's scientific search into the race of man, cites Charlus as one of Proust's more unacceptable "extravagances," both in his generally degenerate life style and in his particularly inverted tastes: "Few of us have known people so distinguished and so depraved as Charlus. . . . Proust would seem to be working with a set of characters so prone to homosexuality as to compromise the value and appeal of the novel" (Shattuck *Marcel Proust* 54). While Shattuck is not alone in this belief,[17] other, perhaps more interesting approaches might be taken in considering the question as to whether Charlus is a compromising distortion or a distilled essence.

Proust's choice of Charlus is in the tradition of Janet's previously cited belief in the importance of studying not only the healthy, but also the unhealthy states of man before he can be understood. For Proust, Charlus also represents not only the laws of a certain species of the human race, but of life itself: "Race sur qui pèse une malédiction et qui doit vivre dans le mensonge et le parjure, puisqu'elle sait tenu pour punissable et honteux, pour inavouable, son désir, ce qui fait pour toute créature la plus grande douceur de vivre" (2: 615). In his inescapable need for dissimulation, Charlus is a microcosm of society in general (Moss 62). Though they must be hidden, the sexual obsessions of this "homme-femme" represent one of the fundamental laws of nature itself: "Ce sont des aspects différents d'une même réalité. Et même celui qui nous répugne est le plus touchant, plus touchant que toutes les délicatesses, car il représente un admirable effort inconscient de la nature" (2: 622). His hidden side is out of the control of his will, his intelligence, his reason, just as a plant is when it follows its basic natural laws: "pourtant en lui, avec quelles ruses, quelle agilité, quelle obstination de plante grimpante, la femme inconsciente et visible cherche-t-elle l'organe masculin!" (2: 621) J. E. Rivers shows that Proust: "used the idea of the 'man-woman' to suggest the androgynous nature of humanity in general. In this Proust was also a man of his time."[18] The concepts of Darwin, Freud and C. G. Jung, along with those of other members of the natural and psychological sciences, "revolved around concepts of androgyny" (228). In fact, as William C. Carter correctly points out, it is the very *lack* of characters who are exclusively homosexual that is striking in

Proust's novel. What Proust is trying to do, in part, is show the essential "mutability of human personality" ("Proust's View" 60-61).

The little enclosed world of Jupien's male brothel provides an ideal source of information concerning this hidden society. Because of the very nature of Jupien's highly clandestine hotel, Proust is provided with an even greater satisfaction when its reality is revealed. It is so secretive as to be considered as possibly subversive, with its members being mistaken for spies. Seeing Charlus enter the brothel, even the narrator is forced to ask himself if Jupien's hotel might be a meeting place for spies (3: 811). Similarly, a heterosexual employee at another hotel, aghast at the amount of money the baron was promising him, at first takes Charlus to be a spy: "Et il s'est senti bien à l'aise quand il a vu qu'on ne lui demandait pas de livrer sa patrie, mais son corps, ce qui n'est peut-être pas plus moral, mais ce qui est moins dangereux et surtout plus facile" (3: 831). Proust's interest in this society certainly may have other causes, but it is also consistent both with Janet's philosophy and with Proust's overwhelming desire to penetrate the veil of a perceived truth in order to arrive at the hidden reality. This is true of his relationship with the enclosed, separate, mysterious world of the aristocracy (represented here by the Baron de Charlus), as well as that of the world of the working man (represented here by Jupien, a former employee of the narrator's family and present owner and maître d'hôtel of the brothel). The suggestion of another perspective to the infinite, of worlds within worlds, of societies within societies, is as clear as this case study's universal application.

Some critics, such as André Maurois, see that characters such as Charlus (or Balzac's Vautrin) give a certain dark depth to a novel and praise the "dessous inexplorés qui vont au sublime" (275). For Marcel Plantevignes, this penchant for mystery and its revelation was an essential part of Proust's character and beliefs (186). According to Plantevignes, Proust disliked most histories because they were written from an external point of view, leaving out the internal essentials which truly determine an event (358). Proust's enjoyment of such scenes was one of a naturalist describing a new discovery, of an "herborisateur qui en herborisant dans la société a découvert par hasard un cas curieux, un type non encore décrit, non catalogué" (467).

The resulting effects on readers are varied—as one might imagine—ranging from moral indignation to aesthetic questioning. While some critics (such as D. W. Alden) see in these discussions of science and homosexuality an example of Proust's "faux-scientisme," others see a positive, metaphorical fusion of science and myth which forms the essence of the artistic activity: "The story of the narrator's development as an artist could be described as the story of his search for a meeting ground between scientific truth and mythic truth. . . . Science becomes visionary and fantastic; myth becomes analytical and precise. And nowhere is this relationship more evident than in the treatment of homosexuality" (Rivers 221). For Rivers, not only is Proust's novel a description of a particular individual's life, it is also that of the race of man in general and, as such, requires this uniting of mythic and scientific visions of man and the world. The "man-woman" Charlus is a perfect choice as specimen:

> So in order to recapture lost time in art, in order to make his book a history of the race as well as a history of an individual life, the narrator must rediscover and exploit in his novel something of, on the mythic level, the androgyny of primal humanity and, on the scientific level, the hermaphroditism of the first plants and animals; and then he must show how the two relate. This he does in *Sodome I* in the . . . courtship of Charlus and Jupien. . . . (236)

Rivers, then, denigrates neither Proust's effort to unite science and myth (as does Alden) nor his choice of Charlus as a particular specimen representing the human species in general (as does Shattuck). Proust's "pseudo-scientific" discussion of homosexuality reflects "the puzzle of recognition, the puzzle of memory, the puzzle of heredity. And these, taken together, represent the greatest puzzle of all—the puzzle of the past" (226). It is in the very metaphoricity of these passages that Rivers sees the essential artistic value of the text:

> Establishing, if only fleetingly, the similarity of dissimilars—this is the classic definition of the artist's use of metaphor. And in this sense the new Sodoms and Gomorrahs which coalesce, break up, and re-coalesce throughout *A la recherche* serve as metaphors of the process of metaphor itself, paradigms of the working of that famous linguistic and artistic tool which, more than any other, allows the narrator to unify his book and, through it, his life. (226)

For a number of reasons, then, Proust chooses "the unnatural" Charlus as his specimen in his studies into the nature of the essence of the race of man. As the preceding discussion suggests, and as the following section will show, Proust's attitude in dealing with such a difficult subject is that of a naturalist: distant, objective, amoral, unjudging.

3. The Naturalist

Proust's interest in the science of human natural history is evident throughout *A la recherche du temps perdu*. One has only to look at the title of the second volume, *A l'ombre des jeunes filles en fleurs* to see a general suggestion of the naturalistic direction Proust will follow in his search. The description of Marcel's first sighting of the girls on the beach is assimilated to an insect's view of a plant (here, a geranium): different, seductive patterns perceived in a way not apparent to the normal human observer (1: 789-90). This association of human natural science with that of insects, plants, and animals is fundamental to Proust's philosophy and his novel.

The work of the naturalist Charles Darwin (1809-92) was known to Proust and may have provided the inspiration for these associations. The first specific reference to Darwin appears in *Le Côté de Guermantes*. Oriane (the duchesse de Guermantes)—giving credit to Swann for her knowledge of botany—compares what goes on at night between humans in the Bois de Boulogne to what is going on in the corner of her garden in plain daylight: the latter differing only in its comparative simplicity of consummation. Her somewhat less knowledgeable cousin is unable to appreciate the scientific subtleties of her comparison: "—La commode sur laquelle la plante est posée est splendide aussi, c'est Empire, je crois, dit la princesse qui, n'étant pas familière avec les travaux de Darwin et de ses successeurs, comprenait mal la signification des plaisanteries de la duchesse" (2: 517).

While the role of naturalism is apparent through to the end of the novel, it is in *Sodome et Gomorrhe* that it truly flourishes. On the first page, with the description of a "natural" discovery, Marcel's position is that of a botanist. He has placed himself in such a way as not to disturb any insect that might pollinate the duchess's plant.[19] His position is such that he is also able to observe another chance encounter while remaining unobserved himself. Now, however, it is between two members of the human species: Charlus and Jupien. The stage is set for a naturalistic description of man heretofore not seen in any novel.

According to Darwin, a species originates by descent, with variation, from parent forms, through the natural selection of those individuals best adapted for the reproductive success of their kind. According to

Proust's narrator, "les lois du monde végétal sont gouvernées elles-mêmes par des lois de plus en plus hautes" (2: 603). He goes on to compare the necessity of the fecundation of a flower by an insect to that of a family breeding outside its line. However, this can be carried to an extreme. As there is a need for the sort of homogeneity found in auto-fecundation, so is there the same need for a repetition, a similarity within a family, as within a species. It is a question of balance.[20] These naturalistic reflexions form an integral part of Proust's novel and, if this is not already apparent to the reader, the narrator makes it so: "Mes réflexions avaient suivi une pente que je décrirai plus tard et j'avais déjà tiré de la ruse apparente des fleurs une conséquence sur toute une partie inconsciente de l'œuvre littérature, quand je vis M. de Charlus qui ressortait de chez la marquise" (2: 603).

From his hidden perspective Marcel observes the chance meeting of Charlus and Jupien. The encounter is described in botanical terms, with Jupien's seductive poses reminding Marcel of an orchid trying to lure a bee. It is a "scène préétablie," revealing to Marcel "les lois d'un art secret" (2: 604-05).

The description continues. He loses sight of the bee (Charlus) and—while wondering if Charlus is the bee needed by the orchid, Jupien—ponders the "hasard providentiel" that brought these two together. The scene appears so rooted in the natural sequence of the mating process that Marcel imagines a series of naturalistic transformations, seeing, "successivement un homme, un homme-oiseau, un homme-poisson, un homme insecte" (2: 606). In looking to animals and plants Darwin hopes to discover the laws governing man's biological nature. Conversely, Proust—observing man—sees the predetermined playing out of the same laws that govern the lower orders. They share a fundamental belief in the natural unity of all life.

The most frequent comparison, however, is that of Jupien to an orchid. This particular parallel is an interesting one for two reasons. First, the orchid is one of the showiest and most exotic of flowers. Second, the name orchid comes from the Greek word *orchis,* which also provides the root for compound words referring to testicles (e.g., orchiectomy, or castration). An "herborisateur humain . . . [un] botaniste moral," Marcel feels fortunate to be allowed the chance to observe this particularly unique species (2: 628). In a sentence that suggests the scienfific nature of his description of this rather risqué scene, Marcel makes a somewhat more serious reference to Darwin than that made by the duchess[21]:

> Je trouvais la mimique, d'abord incompréhensible pour moi, de Jupien et de M. de Charlus aussi curieuse que ces gestes tentateurs adressés aux insectes, selon Darwin, par les fleurs dites composées, haussant les demi-fleurons de leurs capitules pour être vues de plus loin, comme certaine hétérostylée qui retourne ses étamines et les courbe pour frayer le chemin aux insectes, ou qui leur offre une ablution, et tout simplement même comparable aux parfums de nectar, à l'éclat des corolles qui attiraient en ce moment des insectes dans la cour. (2: 629-30)

The choice of a homosexual encounter to represent Darwin's theory of natural selection (which depends on those individuals best adapted for the reproductive success of their kind) is, to say the least, paradoxical. A possible explanation is that the survival of the species is not based on as simple a law as that described above. Discussing the psychological games going on between Morel and Charlus in *Le Temps retrouvé*, the narrator suggests that the homosexual relationship serves as a kind of Malthusean braking mechanism for the human race, thereby aiding in its ultimate survival:

> Ainsi le jeu des différentes lois psychologiques s'arrange à compenser dans la floraison de l'espèce humaine tout ce qui, dans un sens ou dans l'autre, amènerait par la pléthore ou la raréfaction son anéantissement. Ainsi en est-il chez les fleurs où une même sagesse, mise en évidence par Darwin, règle les modes de fécondation en les opposant successivement les uns aux autres. (3: 781)

This Malthusean interpretation of the paradox is evident on a larger scale in the description surrounding Marcel's visit to Jupien's male brothel. Here—in wartime Paris—the German airplanes are the insects, and Paris is the flower (3: 801). The a priori restraining effects of the obviously nonreproductive act of the homosexual, as seen on an individual or microcosmic scale in Jupien's male brothel, is equalled (if not eclipsed) by the a posteriori reduction in population incurred during war, as seen on the national or macrocosmic scale here. Neither are judged by Proust from a moral standpoint. They are, rather, described as a natural scientist might.[22] In his inquiry into the natural history of man Proust also asks some fundamental questions concerning the laws governing the hereditary nature of man. The homosexual case offers a perfect vehicle for the (still unanswered) question concerning acquired versus inherited traits. As Rivers points out: "Throughout *A la recherche* the narrator emphasizes the role of heredity in the etiology of homosexuality" (Rivers 159). Could this trait (homosexuality) be passed on from generation to generation and, if so, was it acquired at some point by an ancestor? This is a difficult question, one which is not easily put to experimental verification. Proust, "like the medical theorists of the day . . . vacillates between the idea that homosexuality is an innate condition and the idea that it can be acquired through various external causes . . ." (Rivers 161). Aside from any moral considerations, experimentation on humans (such as those carried on later by the Nazis) would be impractical. The experiment would take generations to observe. Though other species, such as some reptiles, have a faster reproductive cycle, nearly a lifetime of experimentation is still unavoidable. Proust, therefore, cannot participate in an active way in the newly emerging (predominantly German and Austrian) scientific activity of experimental biology.[23] There is no question, however, that Proust shares this modern scientific attitude. His theories are based on observations made in his world, and they provide the raw data for the narrator's similar activities. The resulting parallels between certain characters in the fictional world of his novel and specific individuals in the real world caused some personal difficulties for Proust.[24]

Though Proust never mentions the French naturalist Jean de Lamarck (1744-1829) by name, he appears to be debating his theory: can characteristics acquired by habit, use, or disuse be passed on to future generations through inheritance? Hypothesizing, confining himself to "l'histoire naturelle," the narrator debates the shared traits of different members of the Guermantes family. If, as seems possible, it is "une famille pervertie," then it is not members such as Charlus and Robert de Saint Loup who show hereditary faults. Rather, it is a heterosexual such as the duc de Guermantes who is the exception (3: 687). In his particular taste for black men, Robert de Saint Loup may be exhibiting an inclination, a trait inherited from some past relation who acquired a similar taste. His activities, then, would not be the result of choice (and therefore open to moral judgment), but of scientific necessity.[25]

While Lamarckism had generally been rejected for the tenets of Darwinism by the turn of the century, certain questions it posed still remained. Briefly, the Lamarckian believes that evolution was cumulative: what an individual passes on to his child is not limited to what he himself inherited from his parent, but can be added to through his own experience. The Darwinian holds that evolution is essentially repetitive. If it were not for random mutations—totally unrelated to evolutionary needs—which every once in a while offer some slight modification which will be preserved by the operation of natural selection, there would be no change, no evolution.[26] Disbelievers in the Darwinian interpretation of "blind chance" as the universal law of Nature include "Einstein [who] made his famous comment 'I refuse to believe that the Creator plays dice with the world' " (*Midwife* 31). Another disbeliever was Henri Bergson, whose own vitalist principles conflicted with Darwinian materialism. Proust's apparent interest in this debate, then, is not an isolated case. It further reflects the sort of fundamental questioning concerning the nature of man and of the origin of species— his own and others—that was going on at that time. Just how serious (both intellectually and emotionally) this question was is perhaps best suggested by a contemporary of Proust, the Austrian biologist, Paul Kammerer (1881-1926). His experiments were "so 'specially exciting' that they 'stirred European biology.' " An obituary article in *Nature*, "which is probably the world's most respected scientific journal, called his last book 'one of the finest contributions to the theory of evolution since Darwin' " (*Midwife* 27, 14). Briefly, Kammerer went to the same Galapagos Islands as did Darwin and found the midwife toad (*Alytes obstetricians*). His papers concerning the experiments on this strange amphibian date from 1906 to 1919. They follow its evolution through several generations, and supply a "proof" for his theories concerning acquired characterics. While his results are Lamarckian, his purpose was, in fact, similar to Darwin's: "by studying the variations of lizards . . . to glean some insight into the causes of these variations . . . and thereby of the origin of the species" (96). The essential difference between Lamarckian and Darwinian theory concerns the nature of the causality involved. Kammerer's midwife toad was supposed to be "proof" of the ability of a parent, reacting to its environment, to pass on acquired traits to its offspring. To a Darwinian, any genetic changes are due to totally random mutations. This brought about many heated debates between Lamarckians and Darwinians, with Paul Kammerer leading the former and William Bates dominating the latter. The story is a long, complicated, and unresolved one. Arthur Koestler makes an interesting case in favor of the verity of Kammerer's experiments. Nonetheless, Kammerer was so involved with these experiments that, with the discovery that he had possibly faked evidence, Kammerer committed suicide, and the Darwinian theory prevailed.

Kammerer's story not only provides an interesting example of the importance these unresolved questions had for the leading biologists, physicists, and philosophers of Proust's time, it also shows the concurrent examining of cause and effect and the role of chance in the determination of man's nature. Proust's own concern with causality (one of the most fundamental laws of the mechanistic world view) has already been noted with regard to the laws of physics. According to Marcel Plantevignes, "Proust était naturellement très friand de tout ce qui était *causalité lointaine,* et lorsqu'il avait pu exactement en découvrir le chemin sinueux et tout parsemé de circonstances imprévues, non seulement il en éprouvait un véritable plaisir d'explorateur social, mais il ne résistait pas au régal pour lui de le conter alentour" (585). While Darwin's evidence is based on observations of his different species from the Galapagos Islands, Proust finds evidence of causality in family resemblances. The hereditary relationship between Robert and Charlus with particular regard to their shared (albeit differently manifested) traits of homosexuality is one example.[27] Though he does not discuss the role of chance in genetic terms, it is clear from his numerous references to "le hasard" that he considers it to be an underlying force behind heredity (2: 601, 07). As the narrator himself writes, with regard to both his novel in particular and life in general, "Il y a beaucoup de hasard en tout ceci . . ." (1: 44). Therefore, though it would seem that Proust has found a causal law in heredity, something in which he can finally find certainty and put an end to his search, how much certainty can he hope to find in a causal law based on chance? Again, Proust shows himself to be quite modern in this paradoxical view, common to both the modern vision of the world (with the discoveries due to relativity and quantum physics) and man (with the discoveries due to research into both the nature of the origin of the species of man and the nature of his unconscious). In physics—on the macrocosmic scale—a Newtonian, causal order seems to be evident. On the microcosmic scale, it is randomness, or the law of probability that is in play. Though there is no evidence that Proust shares Einstein's faith in a God who does not gamble, they are both aware of the fundamental scientific uncertainty underlying both disciplines (that is, physics and biology). The question still continues to plague philosophers of natural science such as Jacques Monod (who won the Nobel Prize for Medicine and Physiology in 1965 for elucidating the replication mechanism of genetic material). The importance of natural science in Proust's novel (alluded to by the narrator in the previously cited passage [2: 603]) and its role in his search for certainty are echoed in Monod's preface to his book *Chance and Necessity: An Essay on the Natural Philosophy of Modern Biology* (also subtitled by the publisher "A Philosophy for a Universe Without Causality"):

> But if the ultimate aim of the whole of science is indeed, as I believe, to clarify man's relationship to the universe, then biology must be accorded a central position, since of all the disciplines it is the one that endeavors to go most directly to the heart of the problems that must be resolved before that of "human nature" can even be framed in other than metaphysical terms.[28]

Proust's interest in natural science, then, is fundamental to the development of his philosophies of man and world, and the novel itself. While the narrator enjoys the final party at the Guermantes with a "satisfaction de zoologiste" (3: 944) his search for certainty must continue beyond the biological nature of man, itself based on an apparently a-causal principle. Having framed his search in naturalistic terms, we now turn inward, to Proust's study of man's psychological nature.

4. The Psychologist

Marcel Proust has defined his novel as "un essai d'une suite de romans de l'Inconscient."[29] That Proust was not only considering man's internal landscape from a philosophical, a metaphysical point of view, but also trying to elucidate psychological laws is evident in his numerous precise references to the same in his novel. While listening to conversations during dinner the narrator is x-raying the mentalities which produced them: "le dessin des lignes tracées par moi figurait un ensemble de lois psychologiques" (3: 719). It is the instinct of the artist that draws the general out of the particular, that sees in the insignificant babbling of social parrots, "les porte-parole d'une loi psychologique" (3: 900). It is "le jeu des différentes lois psychologiques" (3: 781) which aids in the flowering of the human race.

It is true, however, that these precise references occur only in the final volume of Proust's novel, *Le Temps retrouvé.* The term "inconscient" is not used until the third volume, *Le Côté de Guermantes,* and the first reference to it in Proust's correspondence does not occur until 1915 ("Origins" 343). The evolution of Proust's thoughts concerning the nature of man's psyche can be seen in two quotes from his novel, one from the first volume, the other from the sixth, *La Fugitive.* In the first quotation, taken from the end of "Combray" (the first section of the first volume) the narrator's description of memory is purely spatial. He uses geological terms to represent the nature of the formation of memory (much like those used by Darwin in his description of the formation of atolls, which helped prove the age of the earth, giving strength to his theory of evolution): "Tous ces souvenirs ajoutés les uns aux autres ne formaient plus qu'une masse, mais non sans qu'on pût distinguer entre eux . . . sinon des fissures, des failles véritables, du moins ces veinures, ces bigarrures de coloration qui, dans certaines roches, dans certains marbres, révèlent des différences d'origine, d'âge, de 'formation' " (1: 186). In *La Fugitive* one finds the introduction of the role of the fourth dimension of time in his psychological description of memory and its partner, "l'oubli": "Comme il y a une géométrie dans l'espace, il y a une psychologie dans le temps, où les calculs d'une psychologie plane ne seraient plus exacts parce qu'on n'y tiendrait pas compte du Temps et d'une des formes qu'il revêt, l'oubli . . ." (3: 557).

This introduction of time serves to bend the linear view of memory, much as the introduction of this fourth dimension into physics via Einstein's General Theory of Relativity resulted in the curving of the Newtonian view of space (and, with the advent of quantum physics, in micro-space).[30] The narrator uses Marcel's magic lantern as an objective correlative to describe this internal truth: ". . . ma mémoire [était] comme la courbure des projections de ma lanterne magique . . ." (3: 529). As Einstein's theories helped move Euclidean geometry from two ("plane" geometry) and three ("solid" geometry) dimensions into the curvature of his four-dimensional space-time continuum, so do Proust's theories concerning memory—with the introduction of time—result in a new view of psychology: ". . . il faudrait user, par opposition à la psychologie plane dont on use d'ordinaire . . . une sorte de psychologie dans l'espace . . ." (3: 1031). The influence of this theory on Proust's style resulted in one of its most exceptional—and criticized—characteristics, his long, parenthetical comments. As noted earlier, the mathematician Camille Vettard referred to these "phrases-polypes" in defense of a reference to Einstein in his "Dédicace à Marcel Proust." Vettard refers to two of Newton's immediate predecessors to describe how Einstein was forced to abandon the mechanistic frame of reference, surrendering the solid system of references of Galileo and Descartes. He was forced to adopt a new, animated, non-solid system, resembling "filaments continuellement agités en tous sens et qui se tordent comme les bras d'une pieuvre. . . . [Les parenthèses de Proust] introduisent comme une quatrième dimension, que l'on peut dire temporelle, en insérant des souvenirs dans la trame de l'actuelle."[31]

The loss of a fixed frame of reference is as much internal as it is external. Not only is the order in the space-time continuum in flux, affecting the objective set of correlatives, but the subjective apparatus of the self, the single, indivisible, subject is also in doubt: "Le moi est une 'entité verbale' qu'il faut détruire comme le reste des vieilles erreurs" (Czoniczer 67).

The self is seen now as a plurality of selves. This is due to two factors, one having to do with developments in psychology, the other related to changes in physics. First, as Alden points out, it is a reflection of the psychological developments of the times:

> Like an "aliéniste" Proust spied on his characters, hoping to discover from their *lapsi linguae* that other *moi* which they were consciously or unconsciously attempting to conceal. . . . Even granted that he was by nature suspicious, if contemporary psychology had not impressed him with the existence of an "unconscious" or a secondary and tertiary *moi* in individuals, he would not have made such a concentrated effort to penetrate the outer crust of his victims. ("Origins" 352)

Czoniczer concurs, and makes reference to the numerous psychologists and writers of the time referring to this multiplication of the "moi."[32]

The plurality of selves is not only one of a sedimentary layering of levels of consciousness. The Platonic Ideal, having undergone an amoeba-like division with the Socratic "Know Thyself" (and, later, with Descartes's dualistic splitting of man into subject and object, knower and known with his famous "Je pense, donc je suis") has become a futile attempt to arrest time. It is a slip-sliding plurality of selves based on memories of events associated with events taking place in the flux of the space-time continuum. The references to this plurality of selves abound in *A la recherche du temps perdu* and vary from a single temporal division ("le moi que nous avons été" [2: 859]) to an innumerable plurality of selves, such as in the following quotation, where each self must undergo the pain of Albertine's departure: ". . . et ainsi, à chaque instant, il y avait quelqu'un des innombrables et humbles 'moi' qui nous composent qui était ignorant encore du départ d'Albertine et à qui il fallait le notifier" (3: 430).

Memory itself is divided, as we see in Proust's well-known distinction between voluntary and involuntary memory. His distinction, while developed to a point unparalleled in literature, philosophy, or psychology, is not original. In writing of "Théodule Ribot, the prolific psychologist," (502) Douglas Alden, while acknowledging Ribot as "the father of affective memory in France," (503) criticizes another scholar for failing to "emphasize . . . the magnitude of the discussion of affective memory which overflowed from the philosophical journals into literature itself."[33] Once again, Proust's theories—philosophical and psychological—are, in many respects, reflections of the spirit of the times.

As with the distinction between a conscious and an unconscious self, the division between voluntary and involuntary memory serves to remove the subject from the contingencies of a Cartesian, reasoning, logical, linear self and places it in an unconscious, instinctive, non-willed realm, presumably outside the bounds of time and space (". . . je sentais que je touchais seulement l'enveloppe close d'un être qui par l'intérieur accédait à l'infini" [Proust 3: 386]). But what, exactly (if "exactness" is a term that can be applied in the field of psychology), is the nature of this unconscious? Is there *An Unconscious* (we recall Proust's reference to "L'Inconscient"), an indivisible, core Self "below" the slip-sliding uncertainty found in the plurality of selves closer to the surface of consciousness?[34] Before answering these questions, however, it is important to examine how Proust proceeds in his search for this underlying essence. Before judging the value of his theory of the Self, of the Unconscious, we must consider his means of gathering information, his methodology.

There are three types of observation in *A la recherche du temps perdu,* each reflecting a different relationship between the object of observation and the observer. Briefly, they can be described as separation, interaction, and fusion. In the first (separation), the post of observation is clearly defined. The observer is purely a spectator. In the second (interaction), the observer is involved with the observed, the spectator has been drawn into the spectacle. In the third (fusion), there is no distinction between observer and observed, spectator and spectacle, subject and object. In discussing these three different types of observation we shall encounter some of the difficulties shared by both Proust and psychologists in general. We shall consider, in part, both what unites and what distinguishes Proust and Freud. We shall see that this relationship is but a reflection of a larger unity in such seemingly disparate explorative and expressive activities as science and art. Proust's three types of observation also serve to answer the question as to whether he is classical, modern, or post-modern, reflecting as they do, the developments in the history of science of all three world views. We shall see that, in the truest sense of the word, Proust is a "theorist." We shall see suggested a unified theory, a world view uniting man and world, subject and object, finite and infinite, East and West. Finally, we shall consider a resolution of Proust's search for certainty by studying two possible archetypes in *A la recherche du temps perdu,* and how they might be interpreted in light of the first—and only—effort by a psychologist (Carl G.

Jung) and a physicist (Wolfgang Pauli) to give a unified view of the nature of the world and man.

There are three striking examples of the first type of observation in Proust's novel. In order of occurrence they are: when Marcel observes Mlle Vinteuil at her father's house in Montjouvain as she and her girlfriend "celebrate" the death of her father (1: 159-65); when Marcel observes the encounter between Charlus and Jupien in the courtyard of the hôtel de Guermantes (2: 601-32); and when, having followed Charlus into Jupien's male brothel, Marcel observes him chained to a bed (3: 810-24). It should be of no surprise that, in each case, Marcel is hidden from view and the participants have no idea that he is there. This point is made quite clear in each of the three cases. In Montjouvain, Marcel is hidden in the shadows outside Mlle Vinteuil's room: "La fenêtre était entr'ouverte, la lampe était allumée, je voyais tous ses mouvements sans qu'elle me vît" (1: 159). In the courtyard, he is hidden first on a stairway, then behind a window whose shutters are only half shut. He listens, careful not to be discovered by Jupien or Charlus: "J'entendais distinctement, se préparant à partir, Jupien qui ne pouvait me découvrir derrière mon store où je restai immobile jusqu'au moment où je me rejetai brusquement de côté par peur d'être vu de M. de Charlus . . ." (2: 602). In Jupien's brothel, he is able to watch Charlus thanks to a round window whose curtain someone forgot to shut, while remaining undetected in the shadows: "Alors je m'aperçus qu'il y avait dans cette chambre un œil-de-bœuf latéral dont on avait oublié de tirer le rideau; cheminant à pas de loup dans l'ombre, je me glissai jusqu'à cet œil-de-bœuf, et là, enchaîné sur un lit comme Prométhée sur son rocher . . . je vis devant moi M. de Charlus" (3: 815).

While some (including George Painter) see this as a manifestation of Proust's voyeuristic tendencies, others (such as Samuel Beckett and Howard Moss) see here an example of Proust's effort to develop a clear, scientific situation in which to observe the human species in its natural, undisturbed activities. Not only is it important that the spectacle remain undisturbed, but the spectator must have a detached, classically scientific sense of objectivity. In each case, it is made clear that Marcel (whatever the case may have been with Proust himself) is not present at the spectacle in order to satisfy any voyeuristic tendencies. He is also devoid of any moral prejudice towards or emotional involvement with the participants. At the Vinteuil house in Montjouvain he finds himself in his unique position because he has fallen asleep: "étant allé jusqu'à la mare de Montjouvain où j'aimais revoir les reflets du toit de tuile, je m'étais étendu à l'ombre et en-dormi dans les buissons du talus qui domine la maison, là où j'avais attendu mon père autrefois . . ." (1: 159). He stays there only out of fear of being detected: "mais en allant j'aurais fait craquer les buissons, elle m'aurait entendu et elle aurait pu croire que je m'étais caché là pour l'épier . . ." (1: 159). As we have already seen, Marcel is in the courtyard of the hôtel de Guermantes because of his botanical interests. While the motivation is slightly different here, and Marcel's spying has become more purposeful, it is due only to a detached curiosity: "La curiosité m'enhardissant peu à peu, je descendis jusqu'à la fenêtre du rez-de-chaussée, ouverte elle aussi, et dont les volets n'étaient qu'à moitié clos" (2: 602). By the time of the scene at Jupien's brothel Marcel's curiosity has emboldened him to an even more active effort in his spying: "Je marchais vivement dans cette direction et appliquai mon oreille à la porte" (3: 815). This more vigorous attitude, however, still does not show any personal involvement. It was only with a detached suspicion of espionage mixed with curiosity and thirst that Marcel ever entered the establishment:

> L'officier avait depuis un moment disparu quand je vis entrer de simples soldats de plusieurs armes, ce qui ajouta encore à la force de ma supposition [d'espionnage]. J'avais d'autre part extrêmement soif. Il était probable que je pourrais trouver à boire ici, et j'en profitai pour tâcher d'assouvir, malgré l'inquiétude qui s'y mêlait, ma curiosité. (3: 811)

At the same time that one can see an increase in Marcel's (always morally, emotionally, and sexually detached) curiosity, one can also note an increasingly penetrating movement with regard to the staging of the spectacle. In the first instance, he is outside the house, in the yard. In the second, he has moved into the enclosed space of a courtyard. In the third, he has entered the confines of a whole society, itself closed off from the world by Jupien's establishment, and is able to observe the spectacle of Charlus's masochism from a corridor outside the room. Even before he watches Charlus undetected, he is able to observe the other members of the society with the same concern for dissimulation: "Je pus apercevoir sans être vu dans l'obscurité, quelques militaires et deux ouvriers" (3: 811). This sense of having crossed several barriers which keep him from the truth reflects his effort to penetrate the levels of conscious will in order to arrive at the hidden unconscious. The association of a horizontal, labyrinthine penetration to a central point with a vertical movement towards the darkness of the unconscious is an important element of Gilbert Durand's *Les Structures anthropologiques de l'imaginaire: Introduction à l'archétypologie générale,* as we see in this quotation from the section entitled "Le Régime nocturne de l'image":

> ... le but que se proposent les constellations que nous allons étudier ne sera plus l'ascension du sommet mais la pénétration d'un centre, et aux techniques ascensionnelles vont succéder des techniques de creusement, mais ce chemin vers le centre sera ... le sentier difficile, méandreux et labyrinthique, le *dûrohana* que laissent pressentir les images angoissantes du gouffre, de la gorge et de l'abîme.[35]

According to Durand, this movement is representative of the effort to arrive at the quintessential aspect of nature: "... mais c'est dans le *Régime Nocturne* de l'image, par le jeu des emboîtements successifs, que la valeur est toujours assimilée au dernier contenu, au plus petit, au plus concentré des éléments" (316). This sense of penetration is reinforced by the suggestion of even more levels of obfuscation having been explored by Marcel. He has manoeuvred through the streets of a city darkened in order to hide it from the German planes. The imagery is even carried as far outward as the sun and as far inward as the depths of a volcano and the labyrinthine corridors of the métro:

> Cependant l'obscurité persiste; plongés dans cet élément nouveau, les habitués de Jupien croyant avoir voyagé, être venus assister à un phénomène naturel comme un mascaret ou comme une éclipse, et goûter au lieu d'un plaisir tout préparé et sédentaire celui d'une rencontre fortuite dans l'inconnu, célébraient, aux grondements volcaniques des bombes, au pied d'un mauvais lieu pompéien, des rites secrets dans les ténèbres des catacombes. (3: 835)

As suggested by the reference to "secret rites" in the preceding quote, and by previously discussed references to a black, inverted religiosity, this scene is placed in a Western religious context, albeit not a pure, upright sort. The same is true of the scene in Montjouvain where the two friends use Mlle Vinteuil's photograph of her father as a kind of religious object in their sadistic, blasphemous ritual: "Ce portrait leur servait sans doute habituellement pour des profanations rituelles, car son amie lui répondit par ces paroles qui devaient faire partie de ses réponses liturgiques" (1: 162). Like Charlus, Mlle Vinteuil has gone "au bout de la cruauté" (1: 163). She is "l'artiste du mal" (1: 164). While this placing of the participants into a religious context is evident in both passages, it remains true nonetheless that the observations are made from a perspective which is itself not based on any prejudices. There are no admonitions, no moral imperatives. In all three passages, a chance encounter presents a spectacle undisturbed by any involvement on the part of the spectator. The spectacle is allowed to continue in its natural process, allowing a rare look at the human species manifesting (on an individual level) its most hidden side, its sexual and sado-masochistic impulses (which, on the larger, national level, is quite apparent in war). As Durand describes it, this conception of the unconscious is Freudian in nature: ". . . dans le sadisme c'est la libido qui s'emparerait des instincts de mort et les projetterait sur l'objet du désir, donnant ainsi une teinte macabre au plaisir lui-même. L'instinct de mort résiderait dans le désir qu'a chaque vivant de retourner à l'inorganique, à l'indifférencié" (222).

In "The Death of the Spectator," Stephen Toulmin describes the etymology of "theory." It originally comes from "Theoros," the official delegate from the city-state who went to consult the Oracle. From this religious context it came to refer to the official delegate to the Games, who went not as a participant, but only as an observer. It then came to be used simply as a contrast to someone who participates. The abstract noun "theoria" denoted the activity of spectating, observing any activity or process in contrast to intervening, participating, or being an agent. In the final step "theoria" achieved its familiar Aristotelian status. It came to refer to a detached intellectual posture and activity with regard to the study of the world.[36] In all three of these scenes, Proust has taken care to keep Marcel in this privileged position. This is the predominant scientific attitude until, including, and after the time of Descartes and Newton. This attitude is perhaps most clearly defined by Descartes's abstractions, which led to "what we paradoxically call 'modern' science": "What Descartes required us to do was not just to divide mind from matter: more importantly he set humanity aside from nature, and established criteria of 'rational objectivity' for natural science that placed the scientist himself in the position of pure spectator" (209).

As Toulmin points out, however, the notion of a scientist as pure spectator is dead. The earlier ideal of a rational objectivity confronting a causal, linear world is an illusion. A new method of inquiry, a new way of developing and expressing laws concerning both world and man are essential. While this is particularly true in psychology, where the object of observation is the human unconscious, it is also true of the world of physics:

> The most significant novelty in twentieth-century science, generally, has been the fact that scientists have run up against the limits of that

> Cartesian methodology at a dozen different points. As Werner Heisenberg showed us, the required conditions do not fully hold even at the finest level of physical analysis: there, our acts of observation alter the states of the particles we observe. (209)

This involvement of the spectator in the spectacle, with its inherent loss of a certainty based on reason, logic, and objectivity is nowhere more apparent than in Marcel's relationship with Albertine.

As we saw in the chapter entitled "Proust's Scientific Spectacles," the uncertainty of the observer, the lover, Marcel, combined with the uncertainty of the observed, the one loved, Albertine, led to the former doubting the very existence of any causal connecting principle at all. The relationship is a "lesson in relativism." Once involved in the spectacle, the observer, no longer detached, is firmly anchored to the object of observation: "On n'est que par ce qu'on possède" (3: 488). Though every effort is made to hold, to imprison Albertine, she escapes. Like any person, she is not an object. She is an agent and, as such, is not subject to "objective" rules of verification. The mechanistic world view requires the scientist to "observe, analyze, describe, and comment on the happenings in the world of nature *without being drawn into them*" (Toulmin 243). First of all, Marcel is drawn "into" Albertine. The requirement of a rational distancing is destroyed. Second, the object of observation is not an object, it is a dynamic process. Third, both observer and observed are immersed in time and, as such, cannot have the fixed frame of reference necessary for information gathering: "Et enfin, ces changements de temps, ces jours différents, s'ils me rendaient chacun une autre Albertine, ce n'était pas seulement par l'évocation des moments semblables . . . chacune avait fait de moi un homme différent . . ." (3: 487).

We arrive, then, at the third type of observation, where a fusion between subject and object, between observer and observed takes place. In psychological terms, this is referred to as self- or auto-analysis. Having realized the difficulties inherent in any study of the nature of man's unconscious from an external position, from outside the self of an "other," the only recourse left in Proust's endeavor is to look within himself. Freud, reaching the same conclusion, soon realized that true self-analysis is not possible either. Jean-Louis Baudry quotes from Freud's *La Naissance de la Psychanalyse:* "Mon auto-analyse reste toujours en plan. J'en ai maintenant compris la raison. C'est parce que je ne puis m'analyser moi-même qu'en me servant de connaissances objectivement acquises (comme pour un étranger). Une vraie auto-analyse est réellement impossible. . . ."[37]

The first instance of fusing of subject and object occurs in Proust's novel when Marcel tastes the madeleine and herbal tea. While aware that some internal essence is making itself known, Marcel is also conscious of the difficulties inherent in any sort of research he might employ in order to discover its nature. He tastes the mixture: "Un plaisir délicieux [l']avait envahi, isolé sans la notion de sa cause" (1: 45). He asks himself where it came from, what it means, how to seize it? He tries a few more mouthfuls, and realizes it lies in himself. He puts down the cup and turns to his "esprit." The search is now in its hands to find the truth. But how? It is not only a question of looking, but of creating. Freud reaches a similar conclusion. The self is like a slide in a magic lantern. By looking at its projection in a work of art (here, the written word), one can study the nature of the unconscious that produced it: "Il ne saurait y avoir d'auto-analyse qui ne soit écrite. C'est le dispositif d'écriture qui assure la possiblitité de l'auto-analyse" (Baudry 103). This free expression of the unconscious requires a temporary setting aside of conscious will and intellect. As we have seen, each encounter is not willed, it comes about by chance. Each experience forms a part, not of voluntary memory, but of involuntary memory. Baudry sees evidence here that Proust and Freud were more than contemporaries. What involuntary memory was for Proust, free association was for Freud: "L'un comme l'autre surent qu'il n'y avait à rechercher pour comprendre ce que nous sommes que ce qui était déjà incarné dans le corps du temps, et qu'il fallait pour y pénétrer user de ce que l'un nommera 'la mémoire involontaire' et l'autre 'l'association libre' " (Baudry 8).

It is here that we begin to arrive at the nature of the unconscious, at "cet état spécial de la mémoire que nous appelons l'inconscient" (Baudry 45). A work of art—in particular a metaphor—unites an internal, subjective truth of the self with an external, "objective" truth of the world. The unity is not forced, it is an "unité qui s'ignorait, donc vitale et non logique . . . né[e] d'une inspiration, non exigé[e] par le développement artificiel d'une thèse" (3: 161). As we have seen in the encounter with the steeples of Martinville and Vieuxvicq, where Marcel writes for the first time, an unexpected sensation, aroused by an unplanned perception of a particular object results in the creation of a work of art. As the narrator points out later in the novel, any knowledge we have is not of the external world itself, it is of our particular impression of it: "C'est que, chaque fois que nous voulons imiter quelque chose qui fut vraiment réel, nous oublions que ce quelque chose fut produit non par la volonté d'imiter, mais par une force inconsciente, et réelle, elle aussi . . . la connaissance est non des choses extérieures qu'on veut observer mais des sensations involontaires . . ." (3: 166).

The artist is studying the laws of man and nature. His experiments and discoveries are "aussi délicates que celles de la science," and he must be as faithful to these truths as is the scientist (3: 888). What causal law is (or was) to the scientist, the metaphor is to the artist:

> . . . l'écrivain prendra deux objets différents, posera leur rapport, analogue dans le monde de l'art à celui qu'est le rapport unique de la loi causale dans le monde de la science, et les enfermera dans les anneaux nécessaires d'un beau style; même, ainsi que la vie, quand, en rapprochant une qualité commune à deux sensations, il dégagera leur essence commune en les réunissant l'une et l'autre pour les soustraire aux contingences du temps, dans une métaphore. (3: 889)

Approaching this question of the shared activities of the artist and the scientist from the latter's point of view, one is reminded of Proust's description of the experience with the madeleine as J. Bronowski describes the scientific search for order, for unity, for laws. The notion of a single fixed order in the world that a scientist will find and record is a myth. For the scientist neither is it simply a question of looking. He, too, must create:

> The scientist looks for order in the appearances of nature by exploring . . . likenesses. For order does not display itself of itself; if it can be said to be there at all, it is not there for the mere looking. There is no way of pointing a finger or a camera at it; order must be discovered and, in a deep sense, it must be created. What we see, as we see it, is mere disorder.[38]

Seeing an order in nature and expressing it in a work of art as Proust has done reveals the same activity as that of a scientist. Seeing the line and circle suggested by the bottom and top of the madeleine as a reflection of the linear and circular structure of the novel, itself manifesting a view of the world, is no different than Kepler's searching for unity in all nature, or Rutherford and Bohr finding a model for the atom in the planetary system. The scientist and the artist share a fundamental belief in a harmonious universe that will reveal itself in underlying symmetrical patterns, both geometrically and numerically. To Timothy Ferris this belief in symmetry is extremely important. "In Greek, the word means 'the same measure' (*sym,* meaning 'together,' as in *sym*phony, a bringing together of sounds, and *metron,* for 'measurement')" (302). That Kepler's research into the movement of the planets was based on a belief in the music of the spheres is not as bizarre or "unscientific" as it might at first seem. The same may be said for Proust's searching for the essence of the self and the world in such illogical, disparate activities as tasting a madeleine, hearing a piece of music, smelling the varnish of a stairway, seeing some steeples, or tripping over paving stones. His vision, reaching as it does from the smallest, most microscopic detail, to the largest, most cosmic view (with the resulting confusion on the part of the reader [3: 1041]) reflects a similar comprehensive view on the part of the twentieth century scientist: "The late twentieth-century may be remembered in the history of science as the time when particle physics, the study of the smallest structures in nature, joined forces with cosmology, the study of the universe as a whole" (Ferris 335). However, have we not drifted from the discussion of psychology to the discussion of cosmologies? Not at all, for our vision of the world has as much to do with our vision of ourselves as it does with the world external to us: ". . . the cosmogonic speculations told us more about ourselves than about the universe they claimed to describe: All, to some extent, were psychological projections, patterns cast outward from the mind onto the sky, like dancing shadows from a jack-o'-lantern" (Ferris 349). The psychologist, the artist, the physicist, all share a belief in the fundamental interrelatedness of nature, and a dedication to truth. While it may be argued that the artist's emphasis is on a reflection of inner, subjective truth, whereas the scientist's is on external "objective" reality, their activities are indeed fundamentally interwoven: "Science is indeed a truthful activity. And whether we look at facts, at things or at concepts, we cannot disentangle truth from meaning—that is, from an inner order. Truth therefore is not different in science and in the arts; the facts of the heart, the bases of personality, are merely more difficult to communicate" (Bronowski 52-53). Ferris refers to this symmetrical unity of psyche and world as "perhaps *the* complete mystery" (385). It is not difficult to see how this search for a theory which unifies not only the most microscopic and macroscopic events in the physical world but also what takes place inside man can lead to what are generally considered "unscientific" or occult studies. However strange this might seem, it is nonetheless one of the more important realizations to come from developments in modern science: "Over the last few decades the climate in both camps has significantly changed: parapsychological research has become more rigorous, statistical and computerised, while theoretical physics has become more and more 'occult,' cheerfully breaking practically every previously sacrosanct 'law of nature.' "39

This would seem to be the case when Proust writes that he has found the essence of both things and self in the privileged moments where his "special pleasure" has taken him outside the contingencies of time and space, and where intelligence only plays an *a posteriori* role to intuition's *a priori* status, as he explains near the end of his novel. Writers who have lost touch with "les vérités mystérieuses," who only describe the truths of the intellect, lack the depth of those who write first from intuition. The role of intelligence is not to be completely disdained, however:

> Je sentais pourtant que ces vérités que l'intelligence dégage directement de la réalité ne sont pas à dédaigner entièrement, car elles pourraient enchâsser d'une matière moins pure, mais encore pénétrée d'esprit, ces impressions que nous apporte hors du temps l'essence commune aux sensations du passé et du présent, mais qui, plus précieuses, sont aussi trop rares pour que l'œuvre d'art puisse être composée seulement avec elles. (3: 898)

It is here, then, in this fusion of subject and object, that the essence of both man and things is found. This theory does not belong solely to Proust, as can be seen in Elisabeth Czoniczer's quote from Bazaille's *Musique et Inconscience:* "L'inconscient est l'intermédiaire vrai entre nous et le monde qui nous entoure: 'il [correspond] vraiment à une espèce de transition entre la réalité cosmique dont il résume les principaux caractères de richesse et de spontanéité, et la réalité mentale dont il facilite l'action' " (94).

Anne Henry sees the source of the "désintellectualisation" both of self and art in the philosophy of the German romantics in general, and Schelling in particular. The participation of the unconscious in an underlying reality which unites the essence of both self and world finds its source in Schopenhauer's theory of an *Ungrund* and of the world as infinite Will: "La visée de la transparence par l'esprit infini qui se pose en face de soi-même devient chez Schopenhauer pure plongée dans le Vouloir infini, contemplation de l'essence de soi aussi bien que du monde, oubli de la séparation" (*Théories* 86). This itself is part of a whole tradition of German romantics who see here a philosophy of art, uniting self and world in a vitalistic yet quasi-scientific way: "Les théoriciens conservent dans leurs descriptions effusives le schéma général d'une philosophie d'Identité mais l'opposition essentielle s'évanouit, le vitalisme finit par concevoir l'œuvre d'art comme un mouvement quasi biologique qui se prépare hors de la conscience bien qu'il demeure le seul geste signifiant de l'univers" (86). This intersubjective unity is clearly evident in Proust's novel as the narrator describes the artist as belonging to a sort of international, unknown country. While he describes "l'existence irréductiblement individuelle de l'âme," (3: 256) he goes on to state that "Chaque artiste semble . . . comme le citoyen d'une patrie inconnue . . ." (3: 257).

In a chance encounter with some apparently insignificant object, devoid of any intellectual interest, an involuntary sensation is aroused which serves both to unite subject and object and to form the basis for involuntary memory. By uniting past and present this involuntary memory permits an escape from the contingencies of time and space and, through its instinctive expression in a work of art, the essence of both self and world is manifested. The result of this process is a certainty, an acausal connecting principle which is at the same time both found and created.

As we have just seen, Anne Henry has shown that Proust's aesthetic theory was strongly influenced by the philosophy of Schopenhauer. This German romantic also affected Carl G. Jung and is likely the origin of the similarities evident in his theory of archetypes and synchronicity and the particular aspect of Proust's novel being studied here. Gilbert Durand exhibits a similar interest in Jung's theory of archetypes and refers to the superiority of Jung's concepts to those of Freud: "Ces dernières se bornent trop à l'image individuelle, aux accidents de la biographie, alors que l'archétypologie prend en considération des structures imaginaires qui, par-delà l'ontogenèse, intéressent et 'résonnent' dans l'espèce tout entière" (253).

At the beginning of "Synchronicity: An Acausal Connection Principle," Jung draws attention to Schopenhauer's " 'On the Apparent Design in the Fate of the Individual,' which originally stood godfather to the ideas [he is] now developing. It deals with the simultaneity of the causally unconnected, which we call 'chance.' "[40] In his theory of synchronicity, Jung looks at "coincidental" events and tries to organize them into "meaningful dispersions," contrasting them with simply random events. Statistical analysis, of course, participates in a similar activity, but Jung's methodology differs in its use of psychological archetypes as a basis of organization (Jung 34). He defines synchronicity as "a psychically conditioned relativity of space and time" (28). Neither will, nor intelligence, nor reason is relevant to the search, as we saw in each of the Proustian encounters which lead to an experience of the "plaisir spécial." There must be a state "of consciousness which Janet called *abaissement du niveau mental;*

that is to say a certain narrowing of consciousness and a corresponding strengthening of the unconscious . . ." (43). This state of mind serves to allow not only the unconscious, archetypal truths to emerge from the human psyche, it also permits the corresponding underlying forms in nature to reveal themselves, undisturbed by any rationally ordered projection onto it. On one hand, a scientific experiment "consists in asking a definite question which excludes as far as possible anything disturbing and irrelevant. It makes conditions, imposes them on Nature, and in this way forces her to give an answer to a question derived by man" (49). Whereas the mechanistic scientific attitude assumes a unity between reason and intelligence in man's consciousness and a causal order in nature, the Jungian theory of synchronicity compels one "to assume that there is in the unconscious something like an *a priori* knowledge or immediate presence of events which lacks any causal basis" (43-44). In their own way both the mechanistic and the Jungian theories are mysterious: "As Einstein used to say, 'The most incomprehensible thing about the universe is that it is comprehensible' " (Ferris 385). These two world views are not mutually exclusive. The only mistake is in taking the Cartesian and Newtonian laws as the sole rule of the universe. This opinion is also found in Schopenhauer's philosophy:

> Coincidence [Schopenhauer wrote] is the simultaneous occurrence of causally unconnected events. . . . All the events in a man's life would accordingly stand in two fundamentally different kinds of connection: firstly, in the objective, causal connection of the natural process; secondly, in a subjective connection which exists only in relation to the individual who experiences it. . . . (Koestler *Roots* 107)

However, one fundamental difference between these two theories is that, while the mechanistic laws are subject to causal verification, those of synchronicity are not. As Carl Hempel points out, verifiability is a fundamental requirement of a scientific explanation:

> . . . science . . . after all, is concerned to develop a conception of the world that has a clear, logical bearing on our experience and is thus capable of objective test. Scientific explanations must, for this reason, meet two systematic requirements, which will be called the requirement of explanatory relevance and the requirement of testability.[41]

The acausal principle, of course, is not subject to causal verification. The synchronistic event cannot be forced to happen. The theory, therefore, cannot be proven according to this requirement of mechanistic science. This too is the case, however, with modern physics, both on the smallest scale, in quantum mechanics, and in the largest dimension, where relativity reigns. It is, in fact, the nature of all science which (as Gregory Bateson has pointed out) cannot *prove,* it can only *probe.* What one must do, therefore, is look at the "meaningful groupings," at the archetypes, and consider both their essential simplicity, and their universal applicability (two other basic requirements of any law) in all fields where the human psyche and nature come together: in science, in religion, and in art.

Two questions should be answered before returning to Proust's novel in order to consider two of its (possible) archetypes. First, what is an archetype? According to Jung, archetypes "constitute the structure of the collective unconscious. The latter represents a psyche that is identical with itself in all individuals" (Jung 29). An echo of the narrator's comment after tasting the madeleine and herb tea, "Chercher? pas seulement: créer," (1: 45) can be heard in another of Jung's descriptions of archetypes: "... as *a priori* ideal forms, [archetypes] are as much found as invented: they are *discovered* inasmuch as one did not know about their unconscious autonomous existence, and *invented* inasmuch as their presence was inferred from analogous conceptual structures" (59).

The second question to be considered pertains to a possible argument concerning the chronological disparity between Proust's life (he died in 1922) and the publication of Jung and Pauli's *Interpretation of Nature and the Psyche.* The first response has already been given. The common philosophical background lies principally in the work of Schopenhauer. Second, there is evidence that this type of aesthetic was "in the air" during Proust's life, as evidenced by work done by the previously mentioned biologist, Paul Kammerer. In his treatise *The Law of Seriality (Das Gesetz der Serie),* Kammerer presents a theory that is quite similar to the one proffered by Jung and Pauli. Published in 1919, the book is divided into two parts. The first part is of a classificatory nature, and reflects Kammerer's zoological background in the meticulous care he took in gathering and organizing apparently "coincidental" occurrences. He defines a "Serie" as "a lawful recurrence of the same or similar things and events—a recurrence, or clustering, in time or space whereby the individual members in the sequence—as far as can be ascertained by careful analysis—are not connected by the same active cause" (*Roots* 85). In this part of the book he makes no effort to explain the occurrences, he simply, as a scientist, makes note of repetitions: "We have found that the recurrence of identical or similar data in contiguous areas of space or time is a simple empirical fact which has to be accepted and which cannot be explained by coincidence—or rather, which makes coincidence rule to such an extent that the concept of coincidence itself is negated" (86). Kammerer describes a "typology" of non-causal concurrences (numbers, names, situations, etc.), a "morphology" (the number of successive coincidences), a "power" (number of parallel coincidences) and "parameters" (number of shared attributes) (85).

The second part of the book is theoretical. Here Kammerer presents an hypothesis to support the data, and postulates an acausal principle which would complement causality: "In space it produces concurrent events related by affinity; in time similarly related series. 'We thus arrive at the image of a world-mosaic or cosmic kaleidoscope, which, in spite of constant shufflings and rearrangements, also takes care of bringing like and like together' " (86). In this part of the book Kammerer also presents a number of precedents to his theory of periodicity, ranging from "the Pythagoreans' magic seven to Goethe's 'revolving circles of good and bad days', up to Freud—who believed in cycles of twenty-three and twenty-seven days which somehow combine to produce the data of significant events" (87). While all of this may seem strange and, despite Kammerer's background and efforts, unscientific, Jung and Pauli are not alone in accepting it as a valuable piece of work. Einstein, for one, "gave a favorable opinion of the book; he called it 'original and by no means absurd' " (Koestler 87). The consideration, then, of these ideas as reflected in Proust's novel, while they may be "original," are by no means absurd.

The first archetype under discussion here is of a geometric nature, the second, numeric. Both play a fundamental role in the history of man's vision of himself and the world. For the Pythagoreans geometry and numbers were united. They formed the basis of philosophy: "The very term 'philosophy' is Pythagorean in origin; so is the word 'harmony' in its broader sense; and when we call numbers 'figures', we talk the jargon of the Brotherhood."[42] The Pythagoreans believed that "ultimately 'all things are numbers' " (29). It was originally as a Pythagorean that Kepler searched for laws in the movements of the heavens. As Wolfgang Pauli writes in his essay, "The Influence of Archetypal Ideas on Kepler's Theories":

> [Kepler] was fascinated by the old Pythagorean idea of the music of the spheres (which, incidentally, also played no small part in contemporary

alchemy) and was trying to find in the movement of the planets the same proportions that appear in the harmonious sounds of tones and in the regular polyhedra. For him . . . "Geometria est archetypus pulchritudinis mundi" (Geometry is the archetype of the beauty of the world). (*Interpretation* 156)

Both the Pythagoreans and Kepler saw the universe as geometrically and numerically ordered. In geometry, it was the circle and the sphere which dominated man's view of the world: "There is something in the perfect symmetry of spheres and circles which has a deep, reassuring appeal to the unconscious—otherwise it could not have survived two millenia" (*Sleepwalkers* 329). Kepler was so upset at having to give up a circular movement for the orbit of the planet Mars for an elliptical, or oval one, that he declared that all he had left was "a single cartful of dung" (329). For Durand, "*Le cercle,* où qu'il apparaîsse, sera toujours symbole de la totalité temporelle et du recommencement" (372).

The first archetype to be considered is that of the diagram described in the appendix. In the design we see the movement from the line (suggested by the steeples) to the circle (as drawn by the motion of the steeples). Several fundamental themes are described which concern Proust's novel, time, space and the unconscious. The image can be seen in every field of man's effort to describe himself and his world: in science, in religion, and in art. The diagram reflects what Durand refers to as "three great themes" he has encountered in his study of archetypes:

> Trois grands thèmes . . . nous paraissent non seulement constituer les homologues antithétiques des visages du temps, mais encore établir une structure profonde de la conscience, amorce d'une attitude métaphysique et morale. Le schème ascensionnel, l'archétype de la lumière ouranienne et le schème diaïrétique semblent bien être le fidèle contrepoint de la chute, des ténèbres et de la compromission animale ou charnelle. (136)

At the top of the circle, with the steeple (or the arrow, or finger of God [Proust 1: 66]) pointed upwards, towards the infinite of the sky, we also see associated the themes of light, the day and, as we shall see at the end of the description of the movements described here, creation. Durand describes the "psychic cohesion" of certain images and presents this particular constellation as an example: "Par exemple les schèmes ascensionnels s'accompagnent toujours de symboles lumineux. . ." (42). Proust's description of the steeples as "trois oiseaux posés sur la plaine" (1: 181) in the light of the day and as "trois fleurs peintes sur le ciel au-dessus de la ligne basse des champs" (1: 182) after sundown is also part of this constellation. Durand refers to Gaston Bachelard, who sketches "une 'ptéropsychologie' où convergent l'aile, l'élévation, la flèche, la pureté et la lumière" (145). Durand later compares Van Gogh's flowers to the pictoral genre "*Kwaché*—fleurs et oiseaux—de la peinture japonaise et de l'esthétique taöiste" (318). The three steeples also make Marcel think of "trois jeunes filles d'une légende, abandonnées dans une solitude où tombait déjà l'obscurité" (1: 182). The introduction of the three girls can be seen as a suggestion of the sensual aspect of the sensorial experience which, for the artist, can lead him into the depths of his unconscious. All of these themes (verticality, ascension, light, day, God) and images (flowers, birds, girls) are part of an essential dialectic of archetypes:

> Le *Régime Diurne* est donc essentiellement polémique. La figure qui l'exprime est l'antithèse, et nous avons vu que sa géométrie ouranienne n'avait de sens que comme opposition aux visages du temps: l'aile et l'oiseau s'opposant à la thériomorphie temporelle, dressant les rêves de la rapidité, de l'ubiquité et de l'envol contre la fuite rongeuse du temps, la verticalité définitive et mâle contredisant et maîtrisant la noire et temporelle féminité; l'élévation étant l'antithèse de la chute tandis que la lumière solaire était l'antithèse . . . des ténébreux aveuglements des liens du devenir. (Durand 202-03)

In fact, according to Durand, the whole meaning of the *Régime Diurne* resides in this notion of a fall: "On peut même dire que le sens tout entier du *Régime Diurne* de l'imaginaire est pensée 'contre' les ténèbres, de l'animalité et de la chute, c'est-à-dire contre Kronos, le temps mortel" (213). It also represents, then, man's immersion in the passing of time. At the end of the last volume of Proust's novel, *Le Temps retrouvé,* man is described as being on stilts which are "parfois plus hautes que des clochers," and which are placed not in space, but in time (3: 1048). As Durand writes in "Les Symboles Catamorphes": "Pour le bipède vertical que nous sommes, le sens de la chute et de la pesanteur accompagne toutes nos premières tentatives autocinétiques et locomotrices. . . . [La chute] constitue pour la conscience la composante dynamique de toute représentation du mouvement et de la temporalité" (123-24). The fall, of course, is a fundamental symbol of the result of carnal desire in Christian literature. The fall, then, represents not only a physical displacement, it also suggests a moral punishment. According to Durand, it is also associated with the apocalypse and all kinds of sins: "S'introduit dans le contexte physique de la chute une moralisation et même une psychopathologie de la chute: dans certaines apocalypses apocryphes la chute est confondue avec la 'possession' par le mal. La chute devient alors l'emblème des péchés de fornication, de jalousie, de colère, d'idolâtrie et de meurtre" (125).

Does Marcel's encounter with the steeples lead him in the direction pointed at by the "finger of god," to a religious communion with an external, omniscient god? No. In the diagram found in the appendix, the steeple can be seen to metaphorically fall first to a horizontal position, reflecting a contact with the finite world, the world known through perception, through the senses. Marcel has encountered no god, he has a sensorial experience of an object on the same plane. Then, with the experience of the "plaisir spécial," as evidenced in the tasting of the madeleine and herb tea, and in the sighting of the steeples, there is an inversion, a movement towards the "landscape of the self." Here the steeple points (metaphorically) downward, to the infinite of the self, to darkness and night, to Satan and to death. This constellation of images is as cohesive as its ascending antithesis. In "Les Symboles Nyctomorphes," Durand describes the negative valorization of darkness. It is for this reason that "Le diable est presque toujours noir ou recèle quelque noirceur" (99). The unconscious is also associated with darkness: ". . . dans les légendes comme dans les rêveries de l'imagination, l'inconscient est toujours représenté sous un aspect ténébreux, louche ou aveugle" (101). Everything is inverted, including death: "La chaîne isomorphe est donc continue qui va de la revalorisation de la nuit à celle de la mort et de son empire" (248).

Evidence of this part of the movement in the diagram is found in the last volume of *A la recherche du temps perdu, Le Temps retrouvé,* where Marcel follows Charlus into Jupien's male brothel. Spying on Charlus, it is as if he has arrived at the very essence of the nature of the world and man. He has followed the pathology of Charlus's illness to its very end: ". . . [jusqu'au jour] où ce Prométhée consentant s'était fait clouer par la Force au rocher de la pure Matière. . . . Pourtant j'ai peut-être inexactement dit: rocher de la pure Matière. Dans cette pure Matière il est possible qu'un peu d'Esprit surnageât encore" (3: 838).

In the darkness of wartime Paris, Marcel has gone to the end of darkness in this apocalyptic scene. The inversion of the ascending values is reinforced by the term used in French for homosexual, "inverti." The sexuality seen here is also sado-masochistic: ". . . au fond de tout cela il y avait chez M. de Charlus tout son rêve de virilité, attesté au besoin par des actes brutaux, et toute l'enluminure intérieure, invisible pour nous, mais dont il projetait ainsi quelques reflets, de croix de justice, de tortures féodales, que décorait son imagination moyenâgeuse" (840). It must be noted, however, that Charlus's sado-masochistic tendencies are, for him, not only a source of pain, but of pleasure: "En somme son désir d'être enchaîné, d'être frappé, trahissait, dans sa laideur, un rêve aussi poétique que, chez d'autres, le désir d'aller à Venise ou d'entretenir des danseuses" (3: 840). This too is an aspect of the archetypal nature of this part of the diagram. In "Le Régime Nocturne de l'Image," Durand describes the process of inversion:

> Arrêtons-nous donc sur ce si important processus d'inversion et demandons-nous par quel mécanisme psychologique se constitue l'euphémisme qui tend jusqu'à l'antiphrase même, puisque le gouffre transmuté en cavité devient un but et la chute devenue descente se transforme en plaisir. On pourrait définir une telle inversion euphémisante comme un processus de *double négation*. (230)

While Charlus has gone "to the end" of his essential nature and, in a sense, will never find any pleasure beyond that which is described here, the artist will escape the confines of the darkness of the night and of the unconscious. The movement shown in the diagram will continue. The artist will project the essence of the unconscious found in the inverted voyage into the self onto his work of art. Like a magic lantern shining onto a screen or a wall, he will project his discoveries onto the blank canvas, or the white page, or whatever his medium may be, and create. The night has served a purpose. It has undergone a revalorization:

> La nuit s'oppose d'abord au jour qu'elle minimise puisqu'il n'en est que le prologue, puis la nuit est valorisée, "ineffable et mystérieuse," parce qu'elle est la source intime de la réminiscence. Car Novalis saisit bien, comme les psychanalystes les plus modernes, que la nuit est symbole de l'inconscient et permet aux souvenirs perdus de "remonter au cœur" pareils aux brouillards du soir. (Durand 249)

At the end of *Le Temps retrouvé,* Marcel completes the movement of the diagram, metaphorically bringing the steeple back up to the light of creation, in "le jour le plus beau" (3: 887) at the Guermantes' home. The god is now the artist. He has created the word, the work of art. This too is part of the "Régime Diurne de l'Image": "On voit donc que la parole, homologue de la Puissance, est isomorphe dans de nombreuses cultures de la lumière et de la souveraineté d'en haut. Cet isomorphisme se traduit matériellement par les deux manifestations possibles du verbe: l'écriture, ou tout au moins l'emblème pictographique d'une part, le phonétisme de l'autre" (176). His pleasure is not like Charlus's, it is found in the experience of his involuntary memory. As such, it is not chained to the contingencies of the causal order of time and space:

> Je sentais bien que la déception du voyage, la déception de l'amour n'étaient pas des déceptions différentes, mais l'aspect varié que prend, selon le fait auquel il s'applique, l'impuissance que nous avons à nous réaliser dans la jouissance matérielle, dans l'action effective. Et, [je repensais] à cette joie extra-temporelle causée, soit par le bruit de la cuiller, soit par le goût de la madeleine.... (3: 877)

Without the voyage into the darkness of the self, the creative act would not be possible. It is in this sense that one does not only look, one creates, and vice-versa. Inside of each person is a book of signs. The artist's work is similar to that of a translator: "... je m'apercevais que ce livre essentiel, le seul livre vrai, un grand écrivain n'a pas, dans le sens courant, à l'inventer, puisqu'il existe déjà en chacun de nous, mais à le traduire. Le devoir et la tâche d'un écrivain sont ceux d'un traducteur" (3: 890). The laws manifested in this translation have nothing to do with either the mechanistic rules of classical science or those of religious morality, or of critical "bienséances." They are created in solitude, according to their own dark truths:

> Quant au livre intérieur de signes inconnus (de signes en relief, semblait-il, que mon attention, explorant mon inconscient, allait chercher, heurtait, contournait, comme un plongeur qui sonde), pour la lecture desquels personne ne pouvait m'aider d'aucune règle, cette lecture consistait en un acte de création où nul ne peut nous suppléer ni même collaborer avec nous. (3: 879)

The second archetype we shall look at is numerical. It is found at the bottom of the movement of the diagram just described, in the heart of the darkness of the self, in the "book of unknown signs." It is the number "43," and refers to a room number in Jupien's brothel. When Marcel asks for a room, it is "le 43 [qui] doit être libre" (3: 812). Jupien later tells one of his servants to go have "numéro 43" prepared (3: 814). Marcel is led up to the room: "Bientôt on me fit monter dans la chambre 43, mais l'atmosphère était si désagréable et ma curiosité si grande que, mon 'cassis' bu, je redescendis l'escalier, puis, pris d'une autre idée, le remontai, et, dépassant l'étage de la chambre 43, allai jusqu'en haut" (3: 815). Charlus's dream of being chained and beaten needs more "realism," so Jupien sells the wooden bed which was in room 43, and replaces it with an iron one: "Et M. de Charlus tenait tellement à ce que ce rêve lui donnât l'illusion de la réalité, que Jupien dut vendre le lit de bois qui était dans la chambre 43 et le remplacer par un lit de fer qui allait mieux avec les chaînes" (3: 840). There is no sign saying "this is an archetype." There is no explanation given, nor need there be one. The number of times it occurs, and the context within which it is found, suggest such an archetypal role. This impression is reinforced as "43" is found in other instances in art, in science, and in religion.

One of the most interesting occurrences is found in William Faulkner's *Absalom, Absalom!*. While it is found towards the end in Proust's novel, it appears in the first pages of Faulkner's. While it is a spatial reference in Proust's novel, it is a temporal one in Faulkner's. The atmosphere of the room described, however, bears a remarkable resemblance to that of Proust's room 43, which was so disagreeable that Marcel could not remain in it. The demonic references and the allusions to death also recall Proust's scene. Faulkner's description is too lengthy to quote here in its entirety, but a brief, elliptical quote should give a notion of the strikingly similar use of the number 43:

> . . . long still hot weary dead September . . . a dim hot airless room with the blinds closed and fastened for forty-three summers . . . flecks of the dead old dried paint . . . Miss Coldfield in the eternal black which she had worn for forty-three years . . . dead . . . dim coffin-smelling sweet gloom . . . rank smell of female old flesh . . . a crucified child. . . .[43]

Ghosts, man-horse-demons, destruction, death, ogres, and five more references to "43 years" follow in the ensuing pages.

In André Breton's *Nadja*, "43" is found in one of the pictures which make up part of the book. It is the center of a series of superimposed images. It is inside a heart, which is inside Nadja's face, which is inside a hand. No explanation is given for its presence.[44]

In his *Dictionary of Symbols*, J. E. Cirlot explains that, for the Greeks, the first ten numbers are "entities, archetypes, and symbols."[45]

For Plato, they are the essence of harmony, and harmony is the basis for the cosmos and for man. Dividing 43 into its two parts, "three symbolizes spiritual synthesis, and is the formula for the creation of each of the worlds . . . it is associated with the concepts of heaven and the trinity" (232). Geometrically it is represented by the triangle. Four is "symbolic of the earth, of terrestrial space, of the human situation, of the external, natural limits of the 'minimum' awareness of totality, and, finally, of rational organization" (232). Adding four and three together, one arrives at seven: "symbolic of perfect order, a complete period or cycle. It comprises the union of the ternary and the quaternary, and hence it is endowed with exceptional value. . . . It also corresponds to the three-dimensional cross, and, finally, it is the symbol of pain" (233). Is it a coincidence that, while Jupien is asking for "43" to be prepared for Marcel, "7" is ringing for service?

In an appendix to his essay on Kepler, Pauli has included Fludd's treatise on the "Quaternary." In it, Fludd writes, "for, by 3 and 4 is produced the number 7 which formaliter [symbolically] is downright mystical and full of secrets" (230). In the same appendix, Fludd describes the spiritual unity of the number four and God: "this quadratic number is likened to God the Father in whom the mystery of the whole sacred Trinity is embraced" (227).

For Jung, "There is something peculiar, one might even say mysterious, about number" (57). Numbers are (psychologically) irreducible. Number and synchronicity "both possess numinosity and mystery as their common characteristics" (57). He goes on to explain:

> Number helps more than anything else to bring order into the chaos of appearances. It is the predestined instrument for creating order, or for apprehending an already existing, but still unknown, regular arrangement or "orderedness." It may well be the most primitive element of order in the human mind, seeing that the numbers 1 to 4 occur with the greatest frequency and have the widest incidence. (57-58)

Jung defines number "psychologically as an *archetype of order* which has become conscious" (58). In Jung's geometric mandala (similar in form to the diagram described in the appendix) we find a unity of the two archetypes under discussion here: "Remarkably enough, the psychic pictures of wholeness which are spontaneously produced by the unconscious, the symbols of the self in mandala form, also have a mathematical structure. They are as a rule quaternities (or their multiples). These structures not only express order, they also create it" (58).

A unity of the two archetypes of geometry and number can also be seen in the work of the alchemists. While alchemy generally carries the negative connotation of some kind of occult activity whose only purpose was to make gold out of a common metal, a new respect for it is growing among psychologists, artists, and historians of science and religion. Here, in the alchemist's lab, a belief in the interrelatedness of nature and the psyche, as reflected in all the disciplines was the guiding principle. Theirs was a lesson that modern physics is beginning to realize once again. As Koestler writes, "The odour of the alchemist's kitchen is replaced by the smell of quark in the laboratory" (*Roots* 77). It is possible that here, in the alchemist's lab, we may find information which will help in our "translation" of the numerical "sign" we have found in Proust's novel and, thus, in the "internal book of the self."

In his discussion of one alchemist, "Maria the Jewess," who wrote, "Out of the Third comes the One as the Fourth," Jung uses this "cryptic observation" as an example of the fact that "new points of view are not as a rule discovered in territory that is already known, but in out-of-the-way places that may even be avoided because of their bad name" (135). The alchemist's dream of the transmutation of the elements, which can be seen as an object of ridicule, "has turned out to be a veritable gold-mine for the psychology of the unconscious" (135). This is particularly true of the number under study here: "Their dilemma of three and four, which began with the story that serves as a setting for the *Timaeus* and extends all the way to the Cabiri scene in *Faust*, Part II, is recognized by a sixteenth-century alchemist, Gerhard Dorn, as the decision between the Christian Trinity and the *serpens quadricornutus*, the four-horned serpent who is the Devil" (135). In a final effort to elucidate the nature of the two archetypes being studied, we shall follow one vein of this "gold-mine" in the form of the work of the alchemist, Basilius Valentinus. At the same time, we shall consider the possible relevance of an engraving by Albrecht Dürer entitled *Melancholia I*.

In 1624 a translation of Valentinus's *Occulta philosophia* appeared in France under the title *Azoth ou le moyen de faire l'or caché des philosophes*. The term "Azoth" designates "le mercure philosophal." It also corresponds to universal medicine: ". . . il est 'le principe et la fin de tout corps, et qu'il renferme toutes les propriétés cabalistiques, comme il contient la première et la dernière lettre des trois langues matrices, *l'Aleph* et le *Thau* des Hébreux, *l'Alpha* et l'*Oméga* des Grecs, l'*A* et le *Z* des Latins.' "[46]

Of the fourteen engravings found in Valentinus's treatise, one is of particular interest (Lennep 202). In it one finds both the number being considered here, and the circle of the diagram, along with night and day, and symbolic references to geometry. While the number represented is "34," and not "43," this inversion is of no importance here. There is an androgynous figure within the sphere. It represents "cette 'double chose' que le mot *Rebis* inscrit sur la tunique, désigne traditionnellement" (202). The mirror-image of 34 is like one of Janus's two faces. The "34" inscribed in the sphere corresponds to Jupiter, the antidote to Melancholy.

In a chapter entitled "The Androgynous Vision," Rivers describes the sexual ambiguity of a painting by Elstir, *Miss Sacripant,* as "*the* archetypal metaphor" (231). In it he sees "the very origin of the metaphorical impulse" (231). Proust's "men-women" recapture "lost time by evolving the idea of something 'anterior to the practices of . . . civilization' [2: 177]" (235). The androgynous image evident both in the alchemist's etching and in Proust's novel reflects an effort common to both science and myth: to arrive at the origin of man. Referring to a passage in *A la recherche* (2: 629), Rivers points out Proust's allusion to "the Darwinian theory of primal hermaphroditism" (236). Mythically, Rivers argues, the narrator is like an androgynous god:

> In *Le Temps retrouvé* the narrator is like those androgynous creator gods—Protogonos in the Orphic cosmogony, Elohim in certain interpretations of the Bible—who create the universe at the beginning of time. And he is simultaneously like the Adam of the mystical tradition, who regains his androgyny in Paradise at the end of time. In the cyclical Proustian myth the end is the beginning, and the ripening of experience is the inception of creation. (254)

The elements found in Valentinus's engraving are also present in an engraving done by Albrecht Dürer in 1514 (Lennep 298):

> Cette célèbre gravure consacrée à l'un des quatre tempéraments humains, montre l'ange au visage sombre entouré d'objets divers qui, tous, renvoient à la mythologie saturnienne telle qu'elle s'était propagée dans les cercles humanistes de la renaissance. Saturne était le dieu des mélancholiques . . . mais aussi pour les alchimistes, celui du plomb, de la phase au noir (*nigredo*). (Lennep 285)

This engraving also includes the number being studied under its mirror image, "34." The theory behind the engraving was based on "une vision d'un univers où chaque chose était en sympathie, où le microcosme humain était un reflet du macrocosme, [et qui] détermina une conception systématisée de l'individu" (301). Each individual had a god, a planet, an element, etc.: "Ainsi, la mélancholie fut-elle associée à Saturne, sans doute parce que tous deux étaient sombres, noirs" (301). There is a square in the background composed of numbers which, if added up in any direction, yield 34: "Le carré fourni par Dürer, cette *mensula Jovis* dont la somme des chiffres donne 34 en tous sens, correspondait à un talisman reconnu comme étant un antidote aux troubles de la mélancolie, étant donné que Jupiter avait un ascendant sur Saturne" (303). There is also a ladder with seven rungs which would symbolize "les arts libéraux dont la géométrie qui, à la renaissance, fut dévolue à Saturne et considérée comme l'activité mentale dominante" (302). For Proust, being associated with the planet Saturn was another way of saying homosexual, as can be seen when he writes of those "hommes-femmes" whose interests do not lie solely in members of the same sex, but who also enjoy the company of women: "Ils vivent peut-être moins exclusivement sous le satellite de Saturne, car pour eux les femmes ne sont pas entièrement exclues comme pour les premiers . . ." (2: 622).

While the theory of archetypes cannot be proved, it is hoped that this brief effort to probe into the background of these two "signs" in Proust's novel will suggest the richness of their archetypal value. In the union of subject and object, of psyche and world, they suggest an acausal connecting principle, an order, a certainty which has dominated man's vision of the world and himself. Their recreation in Proust's novel suggests not only a certainty based on the instinctive creation of one man's involuntary memory; they reflect a certainty, an essential connection which unites the unconscious order in the psyche of the human race with a symmetry in the surrounding universe.

✦ ✦ ✦

Conclusion

THE PURPOSE OF THIS STUDY has been to describe Proust's search for certainty. As the first chapter shows, critics have approached his novel *A la recherche du temps perdu,* from various scientific viewpoints: botanical, optical, physical, and psychological. The influences the various scientific disciplines had on Proust are apparent on every level of the novel and provide both a historical and a philosophical perspective from which to view it. The narrator's uncertainty and the search that results are basic to all humankind. As Stephen Hawking writes in his conclusion to *A Brief History of Time:* "We find ourselves in a bewildering world. We want to make sense of what we see around us and to ask: What is the nature of the universe? What is our place in it and where did we come from? Why is it the way it is? To try to answer these questions we adopt some 'world picture.' "[1]

While art and science have separate methods of inquiry and expression, both encounter the limits inherent in the gathering of supposed "objective" knowledge. They grow out of a shared need to find (or create) order in an otherwise chaotic universe. The following chapters of this study were arranged in such a way as to show how Proust's novel reflects this search for a comprehensive world view. They concluded with a hypothesis whose purpose is to suggest particular archetypal evidence of the end result of this search. In chapter two ("Proust's Scientific Spectacles") we saw how Proust's references to glass and optics reflect "modern" developments in industry, art, medicine, and theoretical science. They provide a terminology that allows him to express his theories on art, time, man, and world in a "scientific" manner. They also show the basic fallacy of the positivistic world view. While providing new means to probe the nature of man and world, they ultimately show that no certainty can derive from a knowledge whose very foundation (the objective perception of the world ruled by laws based on fixed, references in time and space, and which can be communicated intellectually and without distortion) is in question.

The repeated failure of the positivistic world view to provide any solid ground for certainty is reflected in chapter three, "Proust in Motion." In this chapter the search was shown to lead outward, from the narrator's room to the stars. At each stage in this voyage the narrator encounters the limits in both the Cartesian conception of man and the Newtonian notion of nature. Motion, change, novelty: all are essential to the formation of Proust's "immense edifice of memory," his novel. Each "special pleasure," experienced in a non-willed, sensory contact with something external to him (the magic lantern, the varnish on the stairway, the madeleine, the steeples, etc.), provides him with an involuntary memory. In contrast with a positivistic methodology, involuntary memory provides a kind of knowledge that is not based on a questionable, albeit rational, objective subject observing a phenomenon whose causal laws are equally in question. Each experience in this movement which leads the narrator outward, into the world external to himself, paradoxically forces the narrator back into himself. The essence of the experience is found in the subject, not in the object.

In chapter four, "Proust and the Human Sciences," we saw the search turn inward, toward the observing subject, man. What is his essence? How can it be found? How can it be expressed? Its essence lies in the "special pleasure" experienced in a sensory contact with an external object. Unlike an experiment performed according to positivist methodology, it cannot be willed or caused to happen. It can only be brought about by a chance encounter. It is not the product of rational analysis, but of intuitive creation. Its expression is not in an intellectual treatise, it is in a metaphor.

Therefore, while we have seen evidence of a classical—or positivistic—search in Proust's novel, his narrator is ultimately forced to create a new methodology, a "modern" world view. His predicament reflects that of the newly emerging form of inquiry known as psychology. How, the psychologists also asked, can one arrive at the essence of the self? How can one observe the "real" self of man, his unconscious, without any conscious distortions? As we have seen, what free association was for Freud, involuntary memory was for Proust. Both provide information that is not dependent on any rational, conscious participation on the part of either the observer or the observed. Here, subject and object, observer and observed, man and world are united. For Proust, the contingencies of time and space are replaced by an acausal, atemporal principle. The essence of both man and world is distilled, fixed, and expressed in a metaphor. What causal law is to science, the metaphor is to art and, while the latter cannot, of course, be said to replace the former in the real world, it may be seen as its complement. While Proust's extensive use of metaphor does appear to stand in lieu of scientific certainty and references to laws are found throughout his novel, the narrator's artistic creation is meant, rather, as a homology.

The final pages of this study presented a possible hypothesis of which the diagram presented in the appendix is an illustration. Gilbert Durand, a theoretician of archetypal criticism, offers some strikingly similar observations in his impressive critical work, *Les Structures anthropologiques de l'imaginaire: Introduction à l'archétypologie générale*. His archetypes correspond to the function of metaphor in Proust's novel and serve as a heuristic device for testing the hypothesis. The diagram in the appendix is not presented as archetypal proof (if indeed such proof may be possible). It has proved itself, however, to be an efficient means to summarize what happens in the experience of the "special pleasure," to organize a discussion on the structure of the novel and to organize a discussion of the archetypes. The introduction of the number 43 draws attention to the essential importance of the smallest detail in this world view. While it functions as if archetypes had universal application it does not—cannot—offer proof thereof.

Proust's botanical references—alluded to in part three of chapter three, entitled "The Naturalist"—clearly place the Charlus-Jupien scene in a scientific context. For some critics, these references are exemplary of Proust's excessive (and objectionable) claim to a pseudo-scientific validity. Here, however, they are seen as an essential metaphoric bridge between the need to account for homosexuality and the inability of science to do just that. The metaphoricity of the passage then becomes absolutely necessary to it.

The result of this effort to find a unified world view based on an unshakable certainty resides in the metaphoricity of the archetypes discussed. Proust's search for a unified vision, while teleologically similar to that of the scientist, reaches beyond its boundaries in such a way as to enrich his world view, rather than to render it spurious. It is hoped that, in its own way, this study will offer a new way of seeing the world of Proust's novel, *A la recherche du temps perdu*.

✦ ✦ ✦

Appendix

The Steeples of Martinville and Vieuxvicq: An Archetypal Subject of Infinite Philosphical Importance

Throughout *A la recherche du temps perdu* the narrator is concerned with his ability to find something about which he can write. In the experience with the steeples of Martinville and Vieuxvicq he finds a subject of "infinite philosophical meaning." He encounters the steeples in an outward movement which provides the physical particulars of reality for what could be, without this experience, as unreal as the projection of a magic lantern. Secluded in the darkness of his room, facing even there the uncertainties of a world in motion, Marcel sees "the raised finger of the day," a projection into his darkened room of the light of the external world, of the day:

> Mais à peine le jour—et non plus le reflet d'une dernière braise sur une tringle de cuivre que j'avais pris pour lui—traçait-il dans l'obscurité, et comme à la craie, sa première raie blanche et rectificative, que la fenêtre avec ses rideaux quittait le cadre de la porte où je l'avais située par erreur, tandis que, pour lui faire place, le bureau que ma mémoire avait maladroitement installé là se sauvait à toute vitesse, poussant devant lui la cheminée et écartant le mur mitoyen du couloir; une courette régnait à l'endroit où, il y a un instant encore, s'étendait le cabinet de toilette, et la demeure que j'avais rebâtie dans les ténèbres était allée rejoindre les demeures entrevues dans le tourbillon du réveil, mise en fuite par ce pâle signe qu'avait tracé au-dessus des rideaux le doigt levé du jour. (1: 187)

The church steeple, referred to by the narrator as "le doigt levé de Dieu" (1: 66), can be seen to be a physical embodiment of the "raised finger of the day," suggesting a very real progression in the movement outward in search of order, certainty, filling in the image he has with the physical particulars of reality. The same may be said of his knowledge of and experience with Mme de Guermantes, whose small, inflamed "bouton" at the side of her nose certified her reality, just as, in a play: "un plissement de la robe de la fée, un tremblement de son petit doigt, dénoncent la présence matérielle d'une actrice vivante, là où nous étions incertains si nous n'avions pas devant les yeux une simple projection lumineuse" (1: 175).

Bound in his physical and mental limitations, fixed in a dull world of habit and order, Marcel's experience with the steeples is novel in a number of ways. Novelty is apparent in that the families' walk had been prolonged "fort au delà de sa durée habituelle." The speed of Dr. Percepied's carriage is increased to a speed normally not experienced: "On m'avait fait monter près du cocher, nous allions comme le vent parce que le docteur avait encore avant de rentrer à Combray à s'arrêter à Martinville-le-Sec chez un malade à la porte duquel il avait été convenu que nous l'attendrions" (1: 180).

The stage is set for the arrival of a "plaisir spécial." The novelty and the speed have unsettled Marcel's familiar world, and he has ceased his intellectual (and vocational) search for a "subject of infinite philosophical meaning." It comes about unexpectedly (at a curve in the road) and instantaneously (all of a sudden):

> Au tournant d'un chemin j'éprouvai tout à coup ce plaisir spécial qui ne ressemblait à aucun autre, à apercevoir les deux clochers de Martinville, sur lesquels donnait le soleil couchant et que le mouvement de notre voiture et les lacets du chemin avaient l'air de faire changer de place, puis celui de Vieuxvicq qui, séparé d'eux par une colline et une vallée, et situé sur un plateau plus élevé dans le lointain, semblait pourtant tout voisin d'eux. (1: 180)

The experience of the "plaisir spécial," then, is outside the contingencies of a world fixed in habit, with reason and an external order based on particular objects grounded in particular places, at particular times. The notion of place is altered. The principle of causality is also in question as he experiences the "plaisir spécial" and, as in his experience with the tasting of the madeleine and herbal tea, does not know the origin of it: "Je ne savais pas la raison du plaisir que j'avais eu à les apercevoir à l'horizon et l'obligation de chercher à découvrir cette raison me semblait bien pénible; j'avais envie de garder en réserve dans ma tête ces lignes remuantes au soleil et de n'y plus penser maintenant" (1: 180).

He writes for the first time and, as the little piece is included, a geometric "signification philosophique infinie" is created in the form of a perspective to the infinite, suggested by the Chinese box-like effect of a work inside a work. In the piece, Marcel describes the steeples of Martinville and Vieuxvicq as stark verticals on a horizontal plane. They are in motion. On the horizon, Marcel first sees the two steeples of Martinville: "Bientôt nous en vîmes trois: venant se placer en face d'eux par une volte hardie, un clocher retardataire, celui de Vieuxvicq, les avait rejoints." Minutes pass and, as the carriage speeds along, the steeples seem like three birds, "trois oiseaux posés sur la plaine, immobiles et qu'on distingue au soleil" (1: 181). The effect of relativity can be seen in the change in lighting, caused by the setting sun, the speed of the doctor's carriage, and the changing perspective, caused by the winding road. As he approaches the steeples, in the light of the setting sun, they are like birds. A little later, looking back, with night falling, they are like three flowers, or three girls:

> ... [les clochers] n'étaient plus que comme trois fleurs peintes sur le ciel au-dessus de la ligne basse des champs. Ils me faisaient penser aussi aux trois jeunes filles d'une légende, abandonnées dans une solitude où tombait déjà l'obscurité; et tandis que nous nous éloignions au galop, je les vis timidement chercher leur chemin et, après quelques gauches trébuchements de leurs nobles silhouettes, se serrer les uns contre les autres, glisser l'un derrière l'autre, ne plus faire sur le ciel encore rose qu'une seule forme noire, charmante et résignée, et s'effacer dans la nuit. (1: 182)

The importance of this passage (that is, with the steeples of Martinville) cannot be overemphasized. The narrator has written for the first time. His life has an original, individual meaning. His work has a "signification philosophique infinie." From stasis to motion, habit to novelty, boredom to adventure, death to life, Marcel can be said to have filled in the "trou noir," the "vide" he faced earlier when trying to find something to write about. It is as if he has replaced a linear, strobe-like lens with a circular one, providing him with a revolutionary change in his world view, freeing him from the confining limits of the contingencies of the mechanistic view of time and space.

Combray, previously only an isolated memory, a thin slice in time and space ("comme si Combray n'avait consisté qu'en deux étages reliés par un mince escalier et comme s'il n'y avait jamais été que sept heures du soir" [1: 44]) is now seen in the round, as if one were arriving by train:

> Combray, de loin, à dix lieues à la ronde, vu du chemin de fer quand nous y arrivions la dernière semaine avant Pâques, ce n'était qu'une

> église résumant la ville, la représentant, parlant d'elle et pour elle aux lointains, et, quand on approchait, tenant serrés autour de sa haute mante sombre, en plein champ, contre le vent, comme une pastoure ses brebis, les dos laineux et gris des maisons rassemblées qu'un reste de remparts du moyen âge cernait çà et là d'un trait aussi parfaitement circulaire qu'une petite ville dans un tableau de primitif. (1: 48)

In the experience with the carriage (or automobile) and steeples another perspective to the infinite is added to this circular vision. It, too, is of a geometric nature. He has begun the resurrection of Combray through a chance encounter with an external object, the steeples of Martinville and Vieuxvicq. As Marcel approaches the steeples they are pointed up, a raised finger directing the way to God. However, as we have seen, the help, the grace that Marcel experiences comes not from above, from an external force, but from an internal one, from down in the depths of the self. A similar inversion is apparent in an earlier passage, where Marcel, attempting to find his way in the streets of Paris, looks for a familiar steeple:

> ... l'abside, musculeusement ramassée et remontée par la perspective, semblât jaillir de l'effort que le clocher faisait pour lancer sa flèche au cœur du ciel; c'était toujours à lui qu'il fallait revenir, toujours lui qui dominait tout, sommant les maisons d'un pinacle inattendu, levé devant moi comme le doigt de Dieu dont le corps eût été caché dans la foule des humains sans que je le confondisse pour cela avec elle. (1: 66)

This "arrow aimed at the heart of the sky" is personified and endowed with motion (as in the passage with the steeples of Martinville and Vieuxvicq): "tel clocher de couvent levant la pointe de son bonnet ecclésiastique au coin d'une rue que je dois prendre" (1: 67). The magic of Marcel's memory (albeit of the limited, rational sort) is engaged and his relationship to the world is transformed. Time and space lose meaning, and the arrow, the finger of god—previously pointed upward, into the heart of the sky—is now pointed downward, into the heart of Marcel:

> ... pour peu que ma mémoire puisse obscurément lui trouver quelque trait de ressemblance avec la figure chère et disparue, [je] reste là, devant le clocher, pendant des heures, immobile, essayant de me souvenir, sentant au fond de moi des terres reconquises sur l'oubli qui s'assèchent et se rebâtissent; et sans doute alors, et plus anxieusement que tout à l'heure quand je lui demandais de me renseigner, je cherche encore

mon chemin, je tourne une rue . . . mais . . . c'est dans mon cœur. . . .
(1: 67)

As on tasting the madeleine and herbal tea, Marcel experiences a "plaisir spécial" at the sight of the steeples:

> . . . ce plaisir spécial qui ne ressemblait à aucun autre, à apercevoir les deux clochers de Martinville, sur lesquels donnait le soleil couchant et que le mouvement de notre voiture et les lacets du chemin avaient l'air de faire changer de place, puis celui de Vieuxvicq qui, séparé d'eux par une colline et une vallée, et situé sur un plateau plus élevé dans le lointain, semblait pourtant tout voisin d'eux. (1: 180)

Emptied of its religious meaning, unfixed in the ordered, empirical, mechanistic universe by the unsettling experience of relativity, the "finger" metaphorically falls, pointing now towards "the obscure landscape of the self." The external, physical world has been left for the internal, metaphysical world of the self (which Proust expresses so succinctly in one of his shorter, alexandrine-like sentences): "Je pose la tasse et me tourne vers mon esprit" (1: 45). The science of physics, with its order, its methodology, its fixed laws has been left for the science of psychology, where the usual tools of the scientific trade must be abandoned:

> Je pose la tasse et me tourne vers mon esprit. C'est à lui de trouver la vérité. Mais comment? Grave incertitude, toutes les fois que l'esprit se sent dépassé par lui-même; quand lui, le chercheur, est tout ensemble le pays obscur où il doit chercher et où tout son bagage ne lui sera de rien. Chercher? pas seulement: créer. Il est en face de quelque chose qui n'est pas encore et que seul il peut réaliser, puis faire entrer dans sa lumière. (1: 45)

Proust recognizes the inherent difficulty in this division of the self into observer and observed, rejecting the dualistic Cartesian maxim "Je pense donc je suis." He knows the experience to be real, though he does not know its cause, nor does it follow the rules of the internal, subjective corollary of the objective laws of the mechanistic world—reason, logic: "Et je recommence à me demander quel pouvait être cet état inconnu, qui n'apportait aucune preuve logique, mais l'évidence, de sa félicité, de sa réalité devant laquelle les autres s'évanouissaient" (1: 45). The experience is immediate, outside the contingencies of time, space and logic. Thus the "plaisir spécial" offers a third possible "signification philosophique infinie," taking one out of the external, physical world and into the countryside of the self, a world with a different set of laws unfettered by the confining and isolating cords of a positivistic view of time and space. It is the ultimate voyage, next to death.

To return to the second possible "signification philosophique infinie"—if one looks at the intermediary movement, between the secured, upwardly and outwardly directed "finger of god" and its inversion downward and inward into the world of the self—one can see the first half of another circle being drawn by the falling finger. First it is pointed up, to God, life, light (the sun, the day), the external infinite, and creation. Then, unsettled in the experience of speed with its effects of relativity, the steeple metaphorically falls to the horizontal, pointing to the finite, physical world, made up of the contingencies of time and space. It is through the world of the senses, and through a chance contact with one of the particulars of reality that make it up, that Marcel is thrown into the landscape of the self. The images of the steeples as three flowers and then as three girls serving to reinforce this sensual aspect. The "finger" is now pointed down, toward the infinite of the self, darkness (night), Satan, and death. The movement, however, does not stop here, for the artist must return to the world, recreating it with his new vision in a work of art. The "finger" has returned to the horizontal again, but it is not pointing to the same world. Rather, it is pointed to one recreated under the projection of the imagination of the artist. In this creative flight (reinforced by the images of the steeples as birds), the finger returns to the vertical, pointing to a new god, new life, a new creation. The lines of the steeples have made a complete circle. His vision of Combray has changed from that of a "mince tranche" to that of a circle. If a drawing is made of this movement an interesting geometrical figure is described, as seen by the illustration given at the end of the appendix.

The geometrical design suggested by this movement can be seen to be replicated in Proust's novel in a progression from the particular to the general: from the little madeleine (the lines of its scalloped bottom, the circle of its expansive top) to the work itself (linear, in the sense that it is the life and times of the narrator, circular in that it ends where it began).

The image described here is prevalent throughout the histories of both religious and scientific world views. Striking similarities are also apparent with certain alchemistic images, as seen by the illustrations discussed in chapter four. While it is not possible to offer "scientific proof," its universality undeniably qualifies it as an archetype.

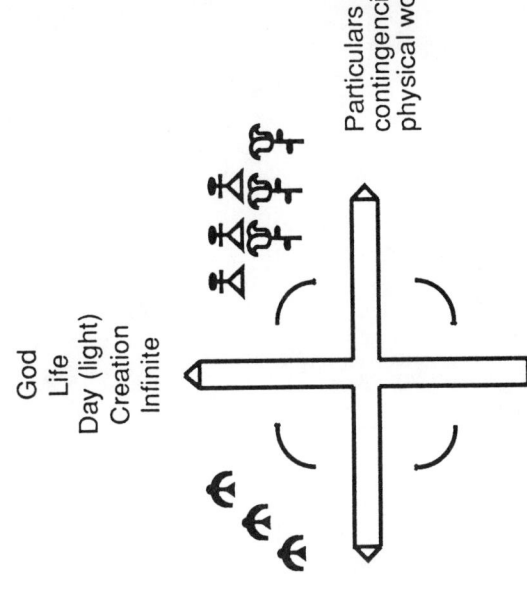

Notes

Introduction

1. J. E. Rivers, *Proust & the Art of Love: The Aesthetics of Sexuality in the Life, Times & Art of Marcel Proust* (New York: Columbia University Press, 1981) 154.

Chapter I

1. Roger Shattuck, *Proust's Binoculars* (New York: Random House, 1963) 6.
2. David Mendelson, *Le Verre dans l'univers imaginaire de Proust* (Paris: Librairie José Corti, 1968) 23.
3. Douglas W. Alden, *Marcel Proust and His French Critics* (Los Angeles: Lymanhouse, 1940) 6.
4. Samuel Beckett, *Proust* (New York: Grove Press, 1931) 68.
5. Serge Béhar, *L'Univers médical de Proust* (Paris: Gallimard, 1970) 15.
6. Alden 52.
7. André Maurois, *A la recherche de Marcel Proust* (Paris: Hachette, 1949) 200.
8. Alden 13.
9. Elisabeth Czoniczer, *Quelques antécédents de "A la recherche du temps perdu": tendances qui peuvent avoir contribué à la cristalisation du roman proustien* (Geneva: Librairie Droz, 1957) 11.
10. Jacques Rivière, *Quelques progrès dans l'étude du cœur humain* (Paris: Librairie de France, 1926) 41.
11. Claude Pichois, *Vitesse et vision du monde* (Neuchatel: Editions de la Baconnière, 1973) 92.
12. Camille Vettard, *Lettres inédites* (Bagnères-de-Bigorre: Maurice Péré, 1926) 127.
13. In Vettard 52.
14. George D. Painter, *Marcel Proust: A Biography* (vol. 2) (New York: Random House, 1959) 2: 336.
15. William C. Carter, "Proust, Einstein, et le sentiment religieux cosmique," *Bulletin de la Société des Amis de Marcel Proust et de Combray* 37 (1987): 52-62.

Chapter II

1. David Mendelson, *Le Verre dans l'univers imaginaire de Proust* (Paris: Librairie José Corti, 1968) 41.
2. See Gregory Bateson's "The Case of Binocular Vision" in his *Mind and Nature: A Necessary Unity* (New York: Bantam Books, 1979) 77-79.
3. Plato, *Cratylus* in John Mansley Robinson, *An Introduction to Early Greek Philosophy* (New York: Houghton Mifflin Co., 1968) 90.
4. Howard Moss, *The Magic Lantern of Marcel Proust* (London: Faber & Faber, 1963) 75.
5. J. E. Rivers, *Proust & the Art of Love: The Aesthetics of Sexuality in the Life, Times & Art of Marcel Proust* (New York: Columbia University Press, 1981) 217-21.
6. Thomas Kuhn, *The Structure of Scientific Revolutions* (Chicago: The University of Chicago Press, 1962) 122.

Chapter III

1. Georges Poulet, *L'Espace Proustien* (Paris: Gallimard, 1963) 93.
2. Antoine Galland, trans. *Mille et une Nuits.* 3 vols. (Paris: Garnier-Flammarion, 1965) 2: 426.
3. George Painter, *Marcel Proust: A Biography* 2 vols. (New York: Random House, 1959) 1: 319-20.
4. André Maurois, *A la recherche de Marcel Proust* (Paris: Hachette, 1949) 308.
5. Marcel Plantevignes, *Avec Marcel Proust: causeries-souvenirs sur Cabourg et le Boulevard Haussmann* (Paris: Nizet, 1966) 166.
6. Paul Morand, *Le Visiteur du soir* (Genève: La Palatine, 1948) 24.
7. Eugène Nicole, "Les Inventions modernes dans *La recherche du temps perdu*," *Bulletin de la Société des Amis de Marcel Proust et de Combray* 36 (1986): 532.
8. Ch. Paul de Kock in Claude Pichois, *Vitesse et vision du monde* (Neuchatel: Editions de la Baconnière, 1973) 18.
9. Roger Kempf, *Mœurs, ethnologie et fiction* (Paris: Editions du Seuil, 1976) 108.
10. Albert Einstein, *Relativity: The Special and the General Theory* (New York: Crown Publishers, 1916) 9.
11. The comparison of these two scenes is not as strange as it may at first seem. As George Painter notes: "for Albert-Jupien's brothel, like the Little Train, was a 'form of society like any other' " (2: 266).
12. Léon Pierre-Quint, *Marcel Proust: sa vie, son œuvre* (Paris: Editions du Sagittaire, 1946) 75.
13. William C. Carter is correct when he states that this passage has been erroneously interpreted by such critics as Margaret Mein, J. E. Rivers, and George Painter as

being based on Proust's experiences with Agostinelli, his driver and secretary. As Carter says, "Le passage où le narrateur voit son premier avion n'a strictement rien à faire avec Agostinelli. . . . La vraie source vécue de ce passage vient d'un autre jeune homme, Marcel Plantevignes. . . ." in "La Mort d'un aviateur," *Bulletin de la Société des Amis de Marcel Proust et de Combray* 38 (1988): 110-11.

14. For more on the airplane-artist symbolism see Carter's previously mentioned article in *Bulletin de la Société des Amis de Marcel Proust et de Combray* 38 (1988): 124. See also Roger Kempf's previously mentioned text, *Mœurs, ethnologie et fiction*.

Chapter IV

1. André Maurois, *A la recherche de Marcel Proust* (Paris: Hachette, 1949) 185.

2. George D. Painter, *Marcel Proust: A Biography* (vol. 1) (New York: Random House, 1959) 60.

3. Roger Shattuck, *Marcel Proust* (New York: The Viking Press, 1974) 142-43.

4. Joyce Megay, *Bergson et Proust: Essai de mise au point de la question de l'influence de Bergson sur Proust* (Paris: Librairie Philosophique J. Vrin, 1976) 16.

5. Anne Henry, *Marcel Proust: théories pour une esthétique* (Paris: Klincksieck, 1981) 77.

6. Georges Poulet, *L'Espace proustien* (Paris: Gallimard, 1963) 135.

7. Philip Kolb, *Correspondance V* (Paris: Plon, 1970) 223.

8. Micheline Tison-Braun, *La Crise de l'humanisme* (Paris: Librairie Nizet, 1967) index.

9. Pierre Janet, *L'Automatisme psychologique—Essai de psychologie expérimentale sur les formes inférieures de l'activité humaine* (Paris: Alcan, 1889) 5-6.

10. Elisabeth Czoniczer, *Quelques antécédents de "A la recherche du temps": tendances qui peuvent avoir contribué à la cristallisation du roman proustien* (Geneva: Librairie Droz, 1957) 31.

11. Léon Daudet, *Devant la douleur—Souvenirs des milieux littéraires, politiques, artistiques, et médicaux de 1880 à 1915*, 2e série (Paris: Nouvelle Librairie Nationale, 1915) 97-98.

12. Douglas W. Alden, *Marcel Proust and His French Critics* (Los Angeles: Lymanhouse, 1940) 77.

13. "Proust's explanation of the psyche makes it almost impossible to deny the validity of something like an indeterminacy principle at the level of individual thought" (Shattuck 104).

14. Marcel Plantevignes, *Avec Marcel Proust: causeries-souvenirs sur Cabourg et le Boulevard Haussmann* (Paris: Nizet, 1966) 383.

15. Serge Béhar, *L'Univers médical de Proust* (Paris: Gallimard, 1970) 124.

16. Howard Moss, *The Magic Lantern of Marcel Proust* (London: Faber & Faber, 1963) 97.

17. For a list of such critics see William C. Carter's article, "Proust's View on Sexuality," *Adam International Review* (1979): 61.

18. J. E. Rivers, *Proust & The Art Of Love: The Aesthetics of Sexuality in the Life, Times & Art of Marcel Proust* (New York: Columbia University Press, 1981) 228.

19. "A défaut de la contemplation du géologue, j'avais du moins celle du botaniste et regardais par les volets de l'escalier le petit arbuste de la duchesse et la plante précieuse exposés dans la cour avec cette insistance qu'on met à faire sortir les jeunes gens à marier, et je me demandais si l'insecte improbable viendrait, par un hasard providentiel, visiter le pistil offert et délaissé" (2: 601-02).

20. ". . . alors, comme une antitoxine défend contre la maladie, comme le corps thyroïde règle notre embonpoint, comme la défaite vient punir l'orgueil, la fatigue le plaisir, et comme le sommeil repose à son tour de la fatigue, ainsi un acte exceptionnel d'autofécondation vient à point nommé donner son tour de vis, son coup de frein, fait rentrer dans la norme la fleur qui en était exagérément sortie" (2: 603).

21. Again, however, the fact that Proust is not a scientist becomes evident in his descriptions of the sexual life of orchids. As Emily Zants points out in her article "Proust's Sexual Fantasia: What Every Proustian Should Know About Cattleyas" (*Proust Research Association Newsletter* 21 [1979]: 11-12), Proust "has strewn the path with botanical references that cannot possibly apply to orchids." The "pistil offert et délaissé" (2: 602) by Jupien does not exist. Orchids have no pistils. Zants mentions several other inconsistencies in his descriptions that show that Proust has obviously combined the sexual habits of several members of the botanical world. The "fleurs dites composées" mentioned in the quote which follows this note is applicable to chrysanthemums, but not to the orchid, which is not a composite flower. This in no way, however, denigrates the arguments presented here. Proust is an artist. He is more interested in the metaphorical development of his creation than any faithful adherence to external particulars. Proust did the same sort of combining of characteristics of people he knew to create the characters in his book. Why should he not do so with plants?

22. The paradox is also evident in the notion of "survival of the fittest" (a phrase that, although attributed to Darwin, actually belongs to Herbert Spencer). Darwin's "third premise—that the differences among individuals, combined with the environmental pressures emphasized by Malthus, affect the probability that a given individual will survive long enough to pass along its genetic characteristics," actually "fits" the unfit Charlus quite well. It is not a question of being physically superior to other members of the species, but of better fitting the environment. "When environmental conditions change, the most exquisitely adapted individuals may suddenly find themselves no longer fit; then it is the freaks and misfits who inherit the future". (Timothy Ferris, *Coming of Age in the Milky Way* [New York: William Morrow and Co., 1988]) 237-38.

23. "Experimental biology was at that time [1903] a new branch of research—a revolutionary break-away from the purely theoretical and descriptive type of zoology taught at the universities." Arthur Koestler, *The Case of the Midwife Toad* (London: Hutchinson & Co. Ltd., 1971) 22.

24. Robert de Montesquiou, for example, took some offense at the possibility of having been the inspiration for the baron de Charlus.

25. "Il est possible que Morel, étant excessivement noir, fût nécessaire à Saint-Loup comme l'ombre l'est au rayon de soleil. On imagine très bien, dans cette famille si ancienne, un grand seigneur blond doré, intelligent, doué de tous les prestiges et recélant à fond de cale un goût secret, ignoré de tous, pour les nègres" (3: 705).

26. "Neo-Darwinism does indeed carry the nineteenth-century brand of materialism to its extreme limits—to the proverbial monkey at the typewriter, hitting by pure chance on the proper keys to produce a Shakespeare sonnet..." (*Midwife* 30).

27. "D'ailleurs, même si les fautes de l'oncle sont différentes de celles du neveu, l'hérédité peut n'en être pas moins, dans une certaine mesure, la loi causale, car l'effet ne ressemble pas toujours à la cause, comme la copie à l'original..." (2: 692).

28. Jacques Monod, *Chance and Necessity: An Essay on the Natural Philosophy of Modern Biology* (New York: Vintage Books, 1971) xi.

29. Douglas W. Alden, "Origins of the Unconscious and Subconscious in Proust," *Modern Language Quarterly* 4 (1943): 343.

30. "*A la recherche du temps perdu* (1913-1927) refléterait la théorie de la relativité d'Einstein, via Bergson et son analyse de la durée, et *Ulysse* (1922), les relations d'incertitude d'Heisenberg et le principe de complémentarité de la mécanique quantique." Didier Anzieu, *Le Corps de l'œuvre* 3 (Paris: Gallimard, 1981) 148.

31. Camille Vettard, *Lettres inédites* (Bagnéres-de-Bigorre: Maurice Péré, 1926) 126-27.

32. "Quant à la multiplicité des moi successifs, quant à la coexistence de deux ou plusieurs caractères dans un seul être, écrivains et psychologues ne cessent d'y revenir. A les citer, on n'a que l'embarras du choix" (69).

33. Douglas W. Alden, "Proust and Ribot," *Modern Language Notes* 58 (1943): 504.

34. A similar effort to posit an indivisible, underlying self can be seen in André Breton's emphasis of "Le Rêve" in contrast to "les rêves."

35. Gilbert Durand, *Les Structures anthropologiques de l'imaginaire: Introduction à l'archétypologie générale* (Paris: Bordas, 1969) 226.

36. Stephen Toulmin, *A Return to Cosmology* (Berkeley: University of California Press, 1985) 239.

37. Jean-Louis Baudry, *Proust, Freud et l'autre* (Paris: Les Editions de Minuit, 1984) 114.

38. J. Bronowski, *Science and Human Values* (New York: Harper & Row, 1956) 13-14.

39. Arthur Koestler, *The Roots of Coincidence* (New York: Random House, 1972) 11.

40. Carl Jung and Wolfgang Pauli, *The Interpretation of Nature and the Psyche,* trans. R.F.C. Hull (London: Routledge & Kegan Paul, 1955) 16.

41. Carl G. Hempel, *Philosophy of Natural Science* (Englewood Cliffs, New Jersey: Prentice-Hall, 1966) 47-48.

42. Arthur Koestler, *The Sleepwalkers: A History of Man's Changing Vision of the Universe* (New York: Grosset & Dunlap, 1959) 27.

43. William Faulkner, *Absalom, Absalom!* (New York: Random House Vintage Books, 1936) 7.

44. André Breton, *Nadja* (Paris: Gallimard Folio, 1964) 144.

45. J. E. Cirlot, *A Dictionary of Symbols*, trans. Jack Sage (New York: Philosophical Library, 1962) 230.

46. Jacques van Lennep, *Alchimie* (Bruxelles: Crédit Communal de Belgique Diffusion Dervy-Livres, 1985) 201.

Conclusion

1. Stephen Hawking, *A Brief History of Time* (New York: Bantam Books, 1988) 171.

Bibliography

Alden, Douglas W. *Marcel Proust and His French Critics.* Los Angeles: Lymanhouse, 1940.
———. "Origins of the Unconscious and Subconscious in Proust." *Modern Language Quarterly.* 4 (1943): 343-57.
———. "Proust and Ribot." *Modern Language Notes.* 58 (1943): 501-07.
Anzieu, Didier. *Le Corps de l'œuvre.* 3 Paris: Gallimard, 1981.

Bateson, Gregory. *Mind and Nature: A Necessary Unity.* New York: Bantam Books, 1979.
Baudry, Jean-Louis. *Proust, Freud et l'autre.* Paris: Les Editions de Minuit, 1984.
Beckett, Samuel. *Proust.* New York: Grove Press, 1931.
Béhar, Serge. *L'Univers médical de Proust.* Paris: Gallimard, 1970.
Breton, André. *Nadja.* Paris: Gallimard Folio, 1964.
Bronowski, J. *Science and Human Values.* New York: Harper & Row, 1956.

Carter, William C. "La Mort d'un aviateur." *Bulletin de la Société des Amis de Marcel Proust et de Combray.* 38 (1988): 102-27.
———. "Proust, Einstein, et le sentiment religieux cosmique." *Bulletin de la Société des Amis de Marcel Proust et de Combray.* 37 (1987): 52-62.
———. "Proust's View on Sexuality." *Adam International Review.* (1979): 56-62.
Cirlot, J. E. *A Dictionary of Symbols.* Trans. Jack Sage. New York: Philosophical Library, 1962.
Czoniczer, Elisabeth. *Quelques Antécédents de* A la recherche du temps perdu: *tendances qui peuvent avoir contribué à la cristallisation du roman proustien.* Geneva: Librairie Droz, 1957.

Daudet, Léon. *Devant la douleur—Souvenirs des milieux littéraires, politiques, artistiques, et médicaux de 1880 à 1915*, 2e série. Paris: Nouvelle Librairie Nationale, 1915.
Durand, Gilbert. *Les Structures anthropologiques de l'imaginaire: Introduction à l'archétypologie générale.* Paris: Bordas, 1969.

Einstein, Albert. *Relativity: The Special and the General Theory.* New York: Crown Publishers, 1916.

Faulkner, William. *Absalom, Absalom!* New York: Random House Vintage Books, 1936.
Ferris, Timothy. *Coming of Age in the Milky Way.* New York: William Morrow and Co., 1988.

Gadamer, Hans-Georg. *Philosophical Hermeneutics*. Trans. David E. Linge. Berkeley: The University of California Press, 1976.
Galland, Antoine, trans. *Les Mille et Une nuits*. 3 vols. Paris: Garnier Flammarion, 1965.

Hawking, Stephen. *A Brief History of Time*. New York: Bantam Books, 1988.
Hempel, Carl. *Philosophy of Natural Science*. Englewood Cliffs, N. J.: Prentice-Hall, 1966.
Henry, Anne. *Proust romancier: le tombeau égyptien*. Paris: Flammarion, 1983.
———. *Marcel Proust: théories pour une esthétique*. Paris: Klincksieck, 1981.

Janet, Pierre. *L'Automatisme psychologique—Essai de psychologie expérimentale sur les formes inférieures de l'activité humaine*. Paris: Alcan, 1889.
Jung, Carl, and Wolfgang Pauli. *The Interpretation of Nature and the Psyche*. Trans. R. F. C. Hull. London: Routledge & Kegan Paul, 1955.

Kempf, Roger. *Mœurs, ethnologie et fiction*. Paris: Editions du Seuil, 1976.
Koestler, Arthur. *The Case of the Midwife Toad*. London: Hutchinson, 1971.
———. *The Roots of Coincidence*. New York: Random House, 1972.
———. *The Sleepwalkers: A History of Man's Changing Vision of the Universe*. New York: Grosset & Dunlap, 1959.
Kolb, Philip. *Marcel Proust: Correspondance*. Paris: Plon, 1970.
Kuhn, Thomas. *The Structure of Scientific Revolutions*. Chicago: The University of Chicago Press, 1962.

Lennep, Jacques van. *Alchimie*. Bruxelles: Crédit Communal de Belgique—Diffusion Dervy-Livres, 1985.

Maurois, André. *A la recherche de Marcel Proust*. Paris: Hachette, 1949.
Megay, Joyce. *Bergson et Proust: Essai de mise au point de la question de l'influence de Bergson sur Proust*. Paris: Librairie Philosophique J. Vrin, 1976.
Mendelson, David. *Le Verre et les objets de verre dans l'univers imaginaire de Marcel Proust*. Paris: Librairie José Corti, 1968.
Monod, Jacques. *Chance and Necessity*. Trans. Austryn Wainhouse. New York: Vintage Books, 1971.
Morand, Paul. *Le Visiteur du soir*. Geneva: La Palatine, 1949.
Moss, Howard. *The Magic Lantern of Marcel Proust*. London: Faber & Faber, 1963.

Nicole, Eugène. "Les Inventions modernes dans *La recherche du temps perdu*." *Bulletin de la Société des Amis de Marcel Proust et de Combray*. 36 (1986): 528-42.

Painter, George. *Marcel Proust: A Biography*. 2 vols. New York: Random House, 1959.
Pichois, Claude. *Vitesse et vision du monde*. Neuchatel: Editions de la Baconnière, 1973.
Pierre-Quint, Léon. *Marcel Proust: sa vie, son œuvre*. Paris: Editions du Sagittaire, 1946.
Plantevignes, Marcel. *Avec Marcel Proust: causeries-souvenirs sur Cabourg et le Boulevard Haussmann*. Paris: Nizet, 1966.
Poulet, Georges. *L'Espace proustien*. Paris: Gallimard, 1963.

Proust, Marcel. *A la recherche du temps perdu.* Eds. Pierre Clarac and André Ferré. 3 vols. Paris: Gallimard Pléiade, 1954.

Rivers, J. E. *Proust & the Art of Love: The Aesthetics of Sexuality in the Life, Times & Art of Marcel Proust.* New York: Columbia University Press, 1981.

Rivière, Jacques. *Quelques progrès dans l'étude du cœur humain (Freud et Proust).* Paris: Librairie de France, 1926.

Shattuck, Roger. *Proust's Binoculars.* New York: Random House, 1963.
———. *Marcel Proust.* New York: The Viking Press, 1974.

Tison-Braun, Micheline. *La Crise de l'humanisme: le conflit de l'individu et de la société dans la littérature française moderne.* 2 vols. Paris: Librairie Nizet, 1967.

Toulmin, Stephen. *The Return to Cosmology.* Berkeley: University of California Press, 1985.

Vettard, Camille. *Marcel Proust: Lettres inédites.* Bagnères-de-Bigorre: Maurice Péré, 1926.

Zant, Emily. "Proust's Sexual Fantasia: What Every Proustian Should Know About Cattleyas." *Proust Research Association Newsletter.* 21 (1979): 11-13.